JAPANESE-STYLE MANAGEMENT: ITS FOUNDATIONS AND PROSPECTS

PROF. RYUSHI IWATA

Asian Productivity Organization

TOKYO

TABLE OF CONTENTS

INTRODUCTION

Over recent years, Japanese-style management has attracted a lot of attention both in Japan and abroad. This reflects, first of all, the worldwide focus on the strength of Japanese enterprises that served as the main driving force for high economic growth during the 1960s. It also signifies another, a more recent appraisal of the vitality of Japanese companies in that, despite the serious setbacks caused by the 1973 oil crisis and the subsequent recession, they were able to show a strong resistance and recuperative power that were not displayed by American and European industries.

It goes without saying that the system of Japanese-style management is not the sole factor that deserves credit for this outcome. In discussing this phenomenon, one cannot ignore certain aspects of the "Japanese" philosophy held by entrepreneurs and employers, such as the willingness to sacrifice their personal and short-term interests for the long-term prosperity of the company or the industry, or the relations between the governmental agencies and industries (a non-hostile relationship in Japan) that helped promote and adjust to the changing situation, or the Japanese concept of labour under which people regard work not merely as something painful but more as an instrument through which they hope to attain the goals of self-development and achievement through cooperation. (It is a real pity that in connection with this last point there is a misunderstanding, particularly among the Europeans, that "the Japanese work blindly under the command of their superiors". Actually, in a sense, the Japanese are involved in organizational activities in a more voluntary and active manner than Westerners.) Having mentioned these elements, the system of Japanese-style still remains the major factor.

Another reason for the increasing interest in Japanese-style management is the fact that the conventional systems of Japanese management have recently come to face many difficulties and are being forced to devise new counter-measures, the question of a higher retirement age being a good example. This, of course, has been brought about by the slowdown of economic growth, aging of the society, and other socio-economic conditions prevailing in the world today. Along with a number of other factors, these circumstances have generated an active exchange of opinions regarding the system of Japanese management.

Since the end of the Second World War, the overwhelming majority of Japanese authorities on business management have been under the predominant influence of American management theories. There have been very few researchers who have even tried to analyze and theorize the realities of Japanese-style management. Such studies have not totalled more than half-a-dozen to date. Furthermore, since they remained under the strong influence of American management theories, until very recently most of the scholars regarded Japanese-style management as being backward and urgently in need of a reform since it differed in many points with the American system.

This attitude was drastically changed during the 1970s. The present book and my previous work, *Nihon-teki Keiei no Hensei Genri (Formative Principles of Japanese-Style Management)*, were written during this transitional period. The purpose of my first book was to reveal the basic formative principles that give Japanese management its various characteristics and to point out that these principles were designed to conform with the social and cultural elements of Japanese society and thus, far from being backward, they were carefully designed formulas for attaining economic objectives by making the best use of the mentality and orientation of the Japanese people. The book was honoured with the "Cultural Award for Economic Publications", an award sponsored by the Nihon Keizai Shimbun (The Japan Economic Journal) and regarded as one of the most prestigeous awards in Japan given to works on economics and business management.

The present book is a sequel to the first. Whereas the first book was aimed mainly at researchers and focused on the fundamental formative principles of Japanese-style management, this book was written mainly for Japanese businessmen who are still active. It describes the structure and foundations of Japanese-style management, fluctuations in the environmental conditions and its responses to such changes, as well as other specific issues.

Since this book was originally written for the Japanese public, elaborate explanations of facts that are obvious to Japanese businessmen (but may not be so for foreign readers) have been largely omitted. With regard to this point, the translator has been kind enough to add a number of footnotes and supplementary comments in the text for better understanding. The author feels that this has helped greatly to make the English manuscript more accessible to foreign readers. Nevertheless, there is a limit to how much the translator can add and if, despite the excellent work of translation, the foreign readers encounter some difficulties in understanding the contents, it is due to the aforementioned omissions and the responsibility lies obviously with the author himself.

At this point, there are two things which certainly derserve the reader's attention. First, it must be understood that the author prepared this manuscript during the very early days when Japanese-style management was starting to be re-examined. Those were the days when there were still many people who firmly believed in the backwardness of Japanese management. Thus, the author's main concern was directed towards the compatibility between Japanese-style management and the social and cultural factors in Japanese society. Consequently, the social and cultural uniqueness of Japanese society is strongly emphasized in this book. The purpose of such an approach is to recognize a pattern that appears throughout the diversity of reality, and since the pattern is a "pure model" that has been abstracted from reality, it inevitably tends to be somewhat exaggerated. For the Japanese businessman who knows or actually experiences the diversity of reality, there is no problem in using this kind of an analysis. In fact, it helps him to understand the complicated reality.

However, the presentation of such a pattern to foreign readers who may not be sufficiently aware of the diversity of reality in Japanese society can lead to misunderstandings and may lead them to picture a mysterious, and even hideous, image of the Japanese. We must bear in mind that although national traits may differ from one country or one race to another, the differences are only variations among a common species called man. Human beings are capable of understanding each other. The only thing that could prevent that is narrow-mindedness (usually arising out of ignorance) and thinking that one's attitude is the generally acceptable attitude and that the other person's position is an exception.

Secondly, there has been some criticism, mainly from foreigners, that this kind of an approach, namely the technique of stressing the connection between Japanese-style management and its social and cultural foundations, is useless for foreigners since their cultural foundations are completely different. To this, the author has but the following to say. Indeed, the basic structure and mechanism of Japanese-style management have developed in such a way as to conform with the social, cultural, and economic foundations supporting Japanese society. So it is rather doubtful whether Japanese-style management can be transplanted as it is to other countries and still be accepted and function effectively. But, as the Japanese entrepreneurs had in the past eagerly borrowed from the advanced American systems and then went on to develop effective management systems that conformed with the "climate" of Japan, if efforts could be made to take Japanese-style concepts and techniques, e.g. the idea of treating organization members not as "replaceable parts" but as colleagues sharing the same work, and apply them is such a way as to conform with the respective societies, the Japanese experience can be useful overseas as well. For that, nothing is more important than an accurate understanding of the structure, mechanism, and foundations of Japanese-style management. It is the desire of the author that this book be a step towards that goal.

I owe a great deal to my American wife Eileen Baired for the preparation of this manuscript. Not only have the differences in the ways of thinking and minor misunderstandings in our everyday life offered me countless intellectual stimuli, but she has always been ready to support my writing activities despite the hardships she has had to go through living in the unfamiliar environment of a foreign country.

As concerns the translation of the manuscript, I would like to express my heartfelt appreciation to the translator, Maki Hamada. The fact that the English text could be so accurate and readable despite the ambiguity and omissions in the original manuscript and that even delicate nuances peculiar to the Japanese phrases could be conveyed was, I must admit, a pleasant surprise for me.

Last but not least, my deepest gratitude goes to the Asian Productivity Organization (APO), in particular George C. Shen, S. Nazim Zaidi, and Yoshikuni Ohnishi, for making the English publication of this book possible.

Ryushi IWATA

Chapter 1

CONCEPT OF INDIGENOUS MANAGEMENT

1.1 DEFINING "INDIGENOUSNESS" OF MANAGEMENT

The course taken by management science in Japan since the end of World War II can be said to have been a process of "naive" devotion to American theories of management. Because of that, academic interest in the realities of management in Japan has been low, and even what little has been studied in that field has been limited mainly to pointing out the backwardness of Japanese management as compared to the American-style management system, or, trying to figure out ways and means of bringing Japanese realities closer to the American system. Such an approach to research reflects a tradition in Japanese academic studies of being overly concerned with acquiring foreign theories. However, it is also a result of having overlooked the deeply-entrenched "climatic nature" of American business management theories while greatly over-estimating its general applicability. When introducing American business management theories, it would have been preferable to do so after making a careful study of its climatic nature and general applicability. Unfortunately, this was not the case.

At the root of this sort of attitude which is held by many Japanese scholars of management and business critics lie certain views or hypotheses regarding man: essentially, that man's reactions towards various organizational situations do not differ because of cultural or social dissimilarities but are the same, whether he be American or Japanese. If we stop and think about this in a reasonable manner, it is immediately apparent that such an assumption does not fit in with reality. Here, I wish to take up the question of responsibility and authority, as recognized and practised by the Japanese, and which is said to form part of the mentality unique to the Japanese people and making them quite different from the Americans and Europeans. By so doing, I shall attempt to clarify several points; namely, that the Japanese reaction to organizational situations is often quite different from that of a Westerner and thus the aforementioned hypothesis is not tenable; that reflecting these differences in man's reactions, the form in which management assumes in Japanese society is substantially different from what one finds in Western societies; that because of this "indigenousness," so to speak, in the Japanese management system, it is not appropriate to "unconditionally" adopt American-style management methods and theories that naturally reflect the American management climate.

1.1.1 Japanese Awareness of Responsibility and Authority

What must be mentioned first as the basic feature of the concept of "responsibility" as recognized and practised by the Japanese is the fact that there is little awareness of "individual responsibility". This has two significant aspects. One is that because awareness of "individual responsibility" is so minimal, the "scope of responsibility" which each individual must accept is obscure. The other point is that one can witness an exceptionally strong presence of "solidarity of responsibility" among the members of a family, university, private firm, and other types of groups. Even in this case, the "solidarity" of responsibility is not based on a contract or even a clearly defined consensus nor is the scope clearly defined. Rather, the concept here is that the mere fact of belonging to the group puts one in the position of accepting such a joint responsibility, if not willingly then unwillingly.

The second characteristic of Japanese-style responsibility is that people feel a responsibility towards the group to which they belong that is more sensitive and stronger even than their responsibility as a citizen, the latter referring to observance of laws and defending social values of one's civic society. Furthermore, it is also true that within a given organization, the members have a stronger sense of responsibility towards lower-level groups, which are relatively close at hand, than to larger groups further up. This awareness and practice of responsibility is clearly evident among Japanese groups, especially when the members are familiar with each other. However, greater reliance tends to be placed on contracts when unfamiliar persons or non-Japanese are involved. This indeed reflects a characteristically Japanese attitude.

The third characteristic feature may well be called the "responsibility of the stronger". When the weaker element in the group is in trouble or placed in an awkward situation, it is considered natural in Japan that he or she seek succour, and that the "stronger" will be considered as being "irresponsible" should he not respond to and take appropriate measures. What is most intriguing about this form of responsibility, which basically has been brought about by "dependence" (*amae*) on the part of the weak, is that it is accepted to a considerably degree by the "strong" as well.

Similar to the case of responsibility, Japanese attitude towards authority demonstrates distinct characteristics. Whereas the English word "authority", in the broad sense, is defined as "power to influence or command thought, opinion, or behaviour of others", it actually connotes two things, the two aspects being expressed by different words in the Japanese language: (1) *ken'i*, or the influence arising from circumstances, in particular the character, status prestige, or title of the person (close to the English word "power" in the vague sense); and (2) *kengen*, or the right, validated by certain rules or consensus, to issue orders, and which is to be exercised within a defined, limited scope (close to the English word "authority" in the stricter sense). The latter, "authority" (or *kengen*), can be interpreted as a set of rights and power granted to a person to carry out a delegated job and which must be respected, within the defined scope, by both his superiors and subordinates. This authority, which is clearly restricted in scope by objective rules, seems to have an extremely important function in Western societies and particularly in American society for facilitating acceptance of orders. The reason for this may be sought in such factors as the Westerner's contractual mentality, attitudes towards obligations, and personnel practices. Thus, in Western organizations, the authority structure comprises an important element of the management system, so much so that the whole management system is almost synonymous with an "authority system".

The question here is to what extent authority in this sense of the word (*kengen*) has penetrated into the "minds" of the Japanese members of organizations. In my opinion, such awareness of authority has hardly penetrated at all. The following are some examples that demonstrate this.

Case Example 1: The president of a Japanese university wished to have his own seminar-type class. However, this proposal had to be withdrawn, to the dissatisfaction of the president, through persuasion by the dean concerned who felt that the president should devote himself to more important tasks. Now, on a separate occasion, when questions were raised about the involvement of the president in a certain matter, the president seized this opportunity to point out that he did not even have the freedom to hold his own class in order to illustrate how limited the "authority" of a university president was. This statement is justified, to a certain degree, from the viewpoint of actual customs in Japanese organizations. In the Japanese context, one can assume that the freedom of this president — whose quite modest desire of conducting his own seminar is being prevented by the organization — is actually quite restricted. However, according to the Western interpretation of "authority", this manner of thinking is perhaps strange. Because for the president to lack the authority to decide who will be in charge of the various classes is no proof whatsoever

3

that he lacks authority within his scope of work, that is, authority as president. This very Japanese idea that any school president who cannot even control such a trivial matter at his own discretion has no "authority" to speak of, illustrates the tendency among the Japanese to look at "authority" not as something that has been validated by objective rules and that has been given a clearly demarcated scope, but as a power or influential force deriving from the circumstances and, in particular, the character of the person involved, in other words as *ken'i* as opposed to *kengen.*

Case Example 2: The grades of a student who tried out for the graduate school were as follows: English – failing mark, German – failing mark, thesis – satisfactory, interview – satisfactory. The candidate was not accepted. The person who designed and scored the English test felt very uneasy for some while knowing that despite the good marks the student got in thesis and interview, he was turned down because of poor performance in the language tests. At the same time however, this person was also able to find comfort in the fact that it was not the English examination alone which had led to the student's rejection. Here again, we see the uniqueness in the mind of the Japanese with regard to the concept of authority. As far as the author knows, when an American professor drops one of his students, he is doing so on the basis of his authority as a professor, the authority which has been granted to him in recognition of the capabilities he possesses. At the same time, he is convinced that it is up to the student to display his abilities and satisfy the professor. The authority of the professor is clearly recognized in such a situation. However, in the above instance of the Japanese student and Japanese teacher, recognition of such an "authority" hardly exists. It should be noted that this is by no means a rare example, and that the same or similar tendencies are widely recognized among Japanese professors. For example, when a professor knows that the failing mark he is going to give to one of his students will force that student to postpone his graduation, he, as a Japanese, is most likely to suffer terrible psychological remorse.

These two examples seem to suggest that an awareness of authority is extremely weak among the Japanese people whereas in Western organizations this authority plays a crucial role in facilitating the acceptance of orders. Moreover, in Japanese organizations, power and influence (*ken'i*) are accorded greater importance than authority as such (*kengen*).*

---

* To avoid redundance and awkwardness, *ken'i* will be translated as "influence" and *kengen* as "authority" hereafter.

1.1.2 Conditions for Acceptance of Orders

Given an environment in which recognition of authority is extremely low, the next question is how orders and commands are accepted in Japan. This is indeed an interesting subject for discussion because modern business organizations cannot exist unless various commands are accepted by one means or other. To elucidate this question, a few features of Japanese-style management must be examined.

(i) Group Structure of Organizations

In Western societies where importance is attached to the "functions" each individual is to fulfill and where there is a constant attempt at clearly demarcating the duties and responsibilities of each individual, one of the prerequisites for the participation of an individual in a business organization is to predetermine and clearly indicate his job description and scope of responsibilities. For this reason, in Western societies, job description and scope of responsibility must be clearly spelled out before the person is hired. As a result, as is widely known, a "job" to which a person is assigned and for which his responsibility is expressly defined, becomes the basic unit of Western-style business organizations. With this as the basic unit, Western-type companies are designed in such a way that these jobs adequately fulfill the overall management goals, bringing about an efficient operating system.

In contrast to this, with Japanese business organizations, the scope of the job assigned to each individual is not necessarily clearly defined. Work is designed not with the individual's job as the basic unit but is rather farmed out to each section, department, and other units of the workforce. As a result, under the Japanese system, priority is put on "accomplishing" the task assigned to the workforce rather than on the individual employee "performing" his job. This structural mechanism is surprisingly consistent with the characteristic features of the Japanese attitude towards responsibility, namely the vagueness of individual responsibility, the idea of "joint group responsibility", and the strong sense of responsibility towards the smaller, closer group. Conversely, we may expect that such an organizational structure would encounter considerable resistance under the Western practice of "responsibility". This just goes to show how differences in the concept of responsibility are strongly reflected in the type of business organizations. The multi-group structure seen with most of the Japanese organizations has a firm psychological foundation in Japanese society.

(ii) Factors Regulating Acceptance of Orders

In such an environment in which more importance is attached to the accomplishment of a task by a workforce rather than to the performance of a job, the following factors expedite the assumption and execution of work by each member of the organization: (1) the unique sense of responsibility towards the group; and, (2) the reverse side of this first emotion which is the anticipation of obtaining the good will of one's colleagues or the fear of losing such good will. In addition, factors that facilitate acceptance of orders from the boss are: (1) the boss' leadership and other favourable personal traits as well as his personal influence; and, (2) the function that the boss possesses of determining the future of the individual members, as exemplified by the personnel evaluation conducted by him. An elaboration of these factors follows.

Responsibility to the group: As has been described, the priority given to responsibility towards one's immediate small group is an important characteristic of the Japanese attitude to responsibility. Because of the presence of such a type of responsibility, the Japanese, in most circumstances, display their potential capabilities better and can keep on "plugging at it" longer when working in groups than as an individual.

Good will of one's co-workers: The strong sense of responsibility towards one's group is supported by the fact that, for any Japanese member of an organization, the good will of one's co-workers (usually expressed as *nakama* in Japanese, a word with the connotation of "pal", "buddy", "colleague") is vitally important and also by the extremely deep-rooted fear of losing such good will should the group's operating be forced to slow down due to his un-cooperativeness with the group or incompetence. In such a context, if the supervisor adequately exercises leadership and plays a crucial role in determining the direction and actions of the group, the feeling of attachment to the group is expressed at the same time as loyalty to the supervisor.

Personal qualities and influence of the boss: The fact that the Japanese people have little awareness of authority also means that there is little respect for authority as such. Thus, flashing authority and forcing oneself on others will have little effect. In the Japanese organizational setup, the word "authority" is generally used in the negative mood such as in the phrase "lack of authority" (*"kengen ga nai"*), and is rarely used in the active sense such as "I have the authority to ... " This certainly reflects and corresponds to this idea of limited recognition of authority. Therefore, one of the means for a boss in a Japanese organization to see to it that his orders are accepted by his subordinates, is to enhance his personal influence, appeal, and existence. Because of this, managers will do their utmost, day in and day out, to appear as appealing as possible to their staff and to build up good rapport with their subordinates. Consequently, whereas a rather emotionally-neutral management is

6

conducted in American organizations, the managers in Japanese organizations rely heavily on a kind of "emotional relationship" they have established with the staff and thus are required to possess the skill to form and maintain such human relations, more so than the demand for their technical and professional ability.

Influential power to determine the future of the organization members: Another means for the manager to encourage his staff to comply with his orders is to draw upon his right to conduct a work evaluation of his staff members, which will in turn influence their promotion. That is to say that the manager, through the work evaluation system, possesses the power to greatly influence the future of his subordinates. Because of this, even a silent rebuke exercises incredibly strong pressure on the subordinates. As has often been explained, under the lifetime employment system*, the members of organizations run through Japanese-style management methods move up slowly together, a step a year, climbing the organizational ladder in a series of minute, continual promotions. During this process, however, slight differentials emerge bit by bit depending on the results of the personnel evaluation. With time, the individual gap broadens, sometimes to an extent no longer recoverable, and naturally the pressure is felt most strongly by the members themselves. For the Japanese, who are extremely sensitive about their relative positions in an organization, this difference has a very heavy impact to the extent of determining whether a person's life has been a success or a failure.

1.1.3 Japanese Management Climate and "Indigenousness"

As is clear from the foregoing sections, the characteristic attitude of the Japanese towards the concepts of responsibility and authority have brought distinctive structures and methods of management into the Japanese management system. It is, therefore, obvious that it would not be possible to unconditionally introduce into such a management climate Western-style organizational structures, or methods that are supported by such structures. By this, I am referring to, for example, American-style job-classification pay, personnel evaluation, and decision-making. It may well be said that this casts great doubt on the validity of what has been done in the past in the field of management science in Japan, where there

---

* Although it has often been pointed out, and rightly so, that the word "lifetime employment" is misleading because the system is actually closer to "semi-guaranteed employment up to retirement", the term will be used throughout this book for convenience sake and also because it is the closest literal translation of the Japanese term *shushin koyo-sei*. See also Chapter 3, 1-(2).

have been efforts to introduce American management theory to Japan without heeding its "climatic nature". Management today, since it involves mobilizing a large group of human beings and often the size of such human organization is enormous, is closely related to the psychology of the human beings comprising the organization. Therefore, the differences between the unique mentalities governing each society will necessarily give rise to distinctive patterns in the style of management in those societies. So, it is probably justified to say that in each management system of the various nations and regions around the world we can find "indigenous qualities" that reflect that society's culture and social mechanism. However, on the other hand, since management science purports to be scientific, it seeks a "universality" that overcomes this "indigenousness". The quest for this universality has, in the past, yielded many results through the Japanese school of "managerial economics" which studied the monetary aspect of business management with the concept of *Das Kapital* at its base, and through the studies in the field of "modern organization theory" which attempts to establish a general theory of organizations at a lofty abstract level. Although in a more limited sense, the same can be said for the traditional theory of management as well.

However, it is clear even from the preceding simple analysis that American-style theory of management has not been able to display its "universality" under the Japanese management climate. And yet, there have been very few occasions on which studies specifically focusing on the "climatic nature" of American management principles were taken up. As a result of an expanded interpretation of the "universal validity" of American-style business theories, there was a tendency among Japanese scholars to interpret the various aspects of "Japanese-style management" that found no place in the American model as the sign of backwardness in Japanese management, or to indulge in a sort of management principles studies whose ultimate goal was to bring the "Japanese-style management" as close to the "advanced American model" as possible. I have argued that the so-called "Japanese-style management" is one adaptive form of the management system that could only have developed in the Japanese cultural and social environment and that it has shown its efficiency, in its own way, in the Japanese social context. When we are reminded of this fact that a management system considerably different from the Western system has functioned effectively, we cannot help entertaining misgivings about rushing headlong into a quest for universality in management theory without stopping to look at the "indigenous qualities" of the management systems in each society. It would seem to be a more necessary task to conduct a comparative analysis of both systems, clarify the differences, and then develop a theory of an even higher universality that would make it possible to describe each management system in a more or less standardized framework. It is this type of operation that I feel will encourage greater advances of theories in the future.

For this reason, I am convinced that a field of study which might perhaps be referred to as "indigenous management science" should be developed for the management systems of each country so as to define the "indigenousness" of each society's management structure from its connection with the social and psychological foundations. If this were to happen, we could expect a blossoming of a new "American management science", "German management science", or even "Japanese management science" that are quite different from what we thought them to be in the past. And these new studies will give us a deeper insight into this field that goes beyond management science as a mere "exercise in exegesis". Furthermore, comparative management science would go beyond a mere taxonomic listing of structural differences and bear truely significant fruit.

In the following section, I wish to explain my views regarding some points and issues that may be encountered in developing an "indigenous management science".

1.2   TECHNIQUES AND SYSTEMS IN MANAGEMENT
1.2.1 Introduction and Efforts

Since World War II, Japanese management has learnt many techniques of management and control from American management methods. While having obstinately persisted in defending traditional ways for the most fundamental areas of management where the "human" element is deeply involved, Japan has accepted many American-type control techniques into its management system and efforts were constantly made to assimilate them.

Generally speaking, business organizations develop or acquire from external sources various management techniques with a view to effectively attaining their business objectives. Here, these management techniques are usually looked upon as *tools* for attaining the business goals as effectively as possible. Consequently, these management techniques are equipped with the unavoidable nature of being studied from the viewpoint of a "functional and rational" linkage of means and ends. And, in many cases, the process does not permit the intervention of human proclivities and norms. This is reflected by the fact that a group of people which interpreted management merely as a question of techniques emphatically advocated the introduction of American-style management skills and sought to adopt them unconditionally.

Unlike the transfer of industrial technology, the transfer of management techniques was not always accomplished smoothly due to the fact that they are often so closely connected with human proclivities. Very often, they had trouble striking roots in the new environment or were able to do so only after having gone through repeated alterations. Indeed, accounting techniques, as well as market research, advertising, and publicity techniques, frequently established themselves in the new climate smoothly with relatively little resistance since their involvement with human proclivities were only indirect. On the other hand, those techniques that implied deep involvement with the treatment of man most probably met with great resistance that arose out of human proclivities.

Once these management techniques are incorporated compatibly into the overall system, formalized, recognized as a working rule, and then become established in the thought patterns of the members of the organization, they assume the nature of becoming a "system". Rephrased, when a decision is made to adopt a certain outstanding technique, that technique is incorporated into the overall system in such a way that it will be compatible with the other existing management systems. Then, it is officially announced to the members of the organization, calling upon each member to accept the new method as one of the working rules. The employees, who may have been somewhat confused at the outset, eventually get used to it and include it among their working rules as if it were the most natural thing. Having gone through this process, the management techniques strike roots as a management system. In the case of *management* systems, such deliberate means of forming and establishing a system is probably the usual pattern. But there are also other types of systems that go through a different process of establishment. Take the example of driving on the left, the system under which traffic is required to keep to the left in Japan. According to one explanation, left-side traffic became the custom in Japan because it was easier for the *samurai* warriors to assume a defensive position if they kept to the left. Of course, there are other explanations, such as that it is easier to protect one's heart by walking on the left side. Which, if either, of these explanations is correct is not the issue here. Let us say that for one reason or another, the mentality and custom of walking on the left-hand side of the street became widespread. Yet, this still only represents a mentality or custom and has not reached the level of becoming a system as such. But in time, this custom has been incorporated into the country's traffic system, formalized as part of the traffic code to be observed by the citizens, and accepted by the people as a clearly defined working rule, thus turning it into a system. Even this kind of a system which came into being through the formalization of a spontaneously generated custom finds itself being exposed to frequent deliberate alterations. A good example of this is the change imposed on the left-hand traffic system by the system of "pedestrians on the right, vehicles on the left". In such a case, some chaos and incompatibility often occured in the beginning. Still, with time, the confusion subsided and the new system gradually struck roots, completing the steps of a deliberate formation of a system as we have already seen.

1.2.2 Difficulty in Reforming

Once a management system strikes roots, and provided that it has attained a certain level of satisfaction, it will settle into its new place nicely. However, if for one reason or another the system fails to remain at the satisfaction level or if the required level itself is raised by management, reform of the system arises as a new issue. If one takes the position of interpreting management systems as merely techniques, this question of reform is very simple in that the main question is whether the new means are more effective and compatible with the objective. The various difficulties during the establishment process will be dealt with as secondary problems. But reforming an established system is not as simple as all that. As an example to demonstrate this, consider the following problem which many companies have been confronted with over recent years.

Ever since the oil shock in 1973, the Japanese economy has passed through a prolonged period of stagnation. It has been pointed out that Japan, which enjoyed growth and more growth during the 1960s and into the earlier years of the 1970s, has finally plunged into a phase of low growth. Together with this trend, "Japanese-style" management which supported high economic growth in the past started revealing a variety of contradictions.

As is often mentioned, "Japanese-style" management was a form of management that was particularly well suited to a period of high economic growth. Taking advantage of the natural tendency of the Japanese towards groupism, Japanese business organizations are composed of sections, departments, and other units, with each of them formed so as to be a group. Consequently, the various drawbacks arising from swelling of the organization and increasing complexity in the job-and-authority structure, which is a product of rapid corporate expansion, are kept to a minimum and the dynamism of the organization is maintained. Moreover, the growth of a business organization offered its members a feeling of security, group's social prestige, and a status within the organization, all of which the Japanese never stop seeking from the organizations they belongs to. In addition, the rapid expansion of a company made it possible to maintain the low-pyramid structure with regard to the age distribution of its members, thus bringing about a situation whereby, under the Japanese system of age-grade pay scheme*, many young workers with low pay channelled their youthful energy into company activities. This made it possible for the companies to keep their wage costs low.

However, as will be discussed in Chapter 5, "Japanese-style" management has come to reveal a number of contradictions now that low economic growth has become a fact of life. The first serious problem that appeared was the "bloated" structure of the companies as they plunged into recession. Unlike the situation with business organizations in Western societies, since this problem clashed head-on with Japan's lifetime employment system, it ended up being one of the most difficult problems to be solved by Japanese employers. Then came a series of problems brought about by the distortions in the age structure of the corporate members. Together with the transition to the low growth era, what used to be a pyramid-shaped age distribution was turning into a sort of "barrel-shaped" structure. This meant that the population within the organization was aging, signifying an increase in the severance pay costs and higher payroll levels while at the same time there was the threat of decreasing corporate vitality. Furthermore, despite the dramatic increase in the number of people reaching the managerial age, the number of supervisory posts did not expand as much, making the relative shortage of such managerial seats an increasingly grave issue.

1.2.3 Need for a System-theory-oriented Approach

What is extremely interesting here is the fact that these problems which could theoretically be resolved very easily by simply abolishing the systems of lifetime employment and age-grade pay turned out to be the biggest headaches for today's employers. In other words, these issues that are troubling many Japanese enterprises today arise from the fact that although the rapid change in the environmental factors have called for reforms in the "Japanese-style" management system, the reforms are not being implemented as smoothly as they should be. If one takes the position that management is simply a matter of techniques, there should be no reason to prevent reform of these systems in accordance with the needs of the organization. Things are, however, not as simple as all that. Because once a management system finds its place in an organization, everyone — even the employers — will find it quite difficult to change it. So, a very essential part of the problems which many entrepreneurs face today is the rigidity of institutional systems.

---

* The author prefers to use the term "age-grade pay system" for the translation of *nenko-sei* since it is a more accurate representation of the system. It should be noted that what is referred to as "age-grade pay system" in this book corresponds to the term "seniority system" in most other literature.

Why is it, then, that a system which was basically designed and established by man to begin with cannot be easily reformed? This question is dealt with in detail in Chapter 7, but at this point I shall offer three explanations. First, it is conceivable that when a certain system has spread widely and struck roots in a society, the very fact that it has socially settled in would enable the system to display a strong constraining force. Second, each individual system, as a part of the overall system and together with the other systems, comprises an overall conglomerate unit. Therefore, it is easy to imagine that the reform of one system would generate various far-reaching implications for other areas within that institutional conglomerate. Thus, resistance comes from these other parts. Thirdly, some of the systems are bound to be intimately connected with the unique psychological traits recognized among the people in the society. This tendency can be all the stronger in cases where there is a close connection with human affairs, in particular with matters related to personal status. Thus, an attempt at reforming a system sometimes encounters enormous psychological resistance from people. This sort of psychological resistance is different in nature from the perplexity accompanying relatively simple transfer of systems, which is basically a mixture of bewilderment and confusion brought about by the feeling of unfamiliarity. The psychological resistance we are talking about here can have a pervasive impact on the formation process of a system.

At the same time, as the institutional structure of management is something that reflects the thinking of the society which is formed in the course of a long period of time it undergoes very minimal and gradual changes except for moments of upheaval. Therefore, when taking up the subject of management, it is indeed meaningful to study it from the viewpoint of "techniques", but it is equally important, or rather of more vital importance, to look at it and understand it as a system.

1.3 PSYCHOLOGICAL FOUNDATIONS

I define "management system" as follows: "A system deliberately formed to effectively attain the management objectives by means of guiding the human orientation — which is supported by their pscyhological traits — in a certain direction, thus regulating and maintaining orderly human behaviour." Translated into John R. Commons' words, it corresponds to the "working rules" in a going concern. Let us consider a few examples. First, the "lifetime employment system" can be interpreted as one of the working rules governing relations between the company and the members who comprise it. Furthermore, the "age-grade pay system" (more commonly known as the "seniority system" in most other literature) is a working rule that regulates the intra-member status relations within a given company. The "authority system" which is prevalent in the American and European companies (and which I believe to be one of the systems that did not succeed in firmly striking roots in the Japanese business world) can be recognized as a working rule concerning the allocation and execution of work. Similarly, the multi-divisional structure system may also be looked upon as one of the working rules regarding sharing and grouping of work.

1.3.1 Establishment of Management Systems

Figure 1.1 illustrates the formation process of these management systems in individual companies. The top managers (or an agency thereof) seek to implement the most effective and efficient management systems to attain its business objectives. Since these various management systems will interact closely with each other to form an overall corporate system, the creation of any new system must be studied in the context of the potential overall efficiency of that total mechanism. At the same time, however, the reactions of the organization members must also be taken into full account. Needless to say, these members possess certain desires and thought patterns, just as do the top management. The members will act in reaction to the systems established by the top management, but there is no guarantee that they will react in the manner desired by the management. So for the organization to attain its objectives effectively, it must be equipped with management systems that effectively foster order in the reactions of its members and that can bring together these reactions with the aim of accomplishing the objectives.

Because of this fact, we can assume that the top management's concept of man will be strongly reflected in the formation process of management systems and that the organization members' reactions to the systems formulated will serve as feedback information for the next formation of yet another system, influencing it considerably. What is important here is the fact that both the top management and the rank-and-file organization members have formulated their personality in a given society, within a given cultural and social environment. In other words, at the base of the idea that each society gives birth to its own unique management style is the existence of various psychological traits that are recognized among the population of that society, and it is these traits that have a pervasive and lasting impact on the formation of systems.

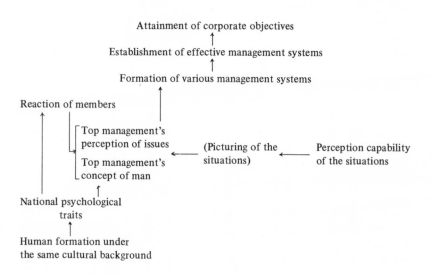

Figure 1.1

The conditions, internal and external, confronted by the individual companies are many and varied. Thus, the perception of issues and problems will also vary among the top managers. Consequently, the various management systems created by each company are quite diversified in their forms and specifics. Nevertheless, reflecting the homogeneity of cultural and social factors among the Japanese companies, we can detect a common pattern in the top managers' concept of man and the organization members' reaction to the systems formulated. Figure 1-2 illustrates the process of how some management systems become widely spread and settled in a society. I refer to the concept or principles underlying the management systems that have struck roots in a society as the "formative principles of management". Those, which have brought about the distinct patterns in Japanese-style management are the formation principles of Japanese-style management. And at its roots are the distinct psychological traits of the Japanese people.

By understanding "management systems" along these lines, I have introduced a number of factors which were not represented, at least specifically, either in Thorstein Veblen's or John R. Commons' studies

15

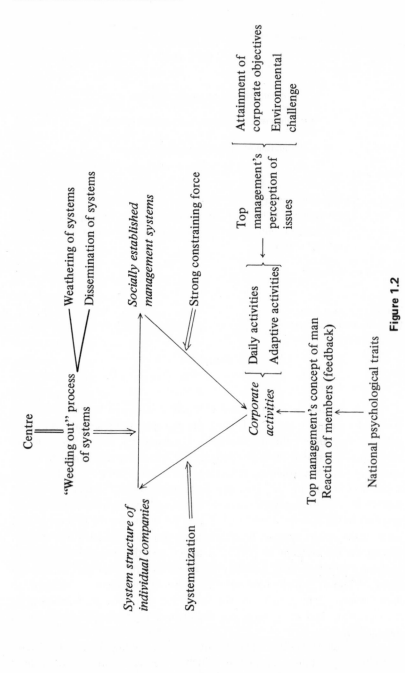

Figure 1.2

on economic systems. These are:

(i) The importance of the factors that exist behind the cumulative transformation process of systems and that persistently seek to realize a certain orientation, i.e. the human psychology, in particular that part which is extremely hard to change.

(ii) As one of the factors that generate the development patterns unique to each social system, in the human psychology described in (i), the role of those national psychological traits readily discerned among the population of the given society.

(iii) Recognizing a distinction between a company and a management system, in that the former is an economic institution while the latter is a customary pattern of thought that has formed and become established within the company. The element of "deliberateness" is very obvious in the latter and its function can hardly be ignored.

1.3.2 Three Categories of Management Systems

When we take the foregoing view of "management system", it would seem appropriate to classify management systems into the following three categories.

(i) This is the case when an existing management system no longer fulfills a satisfactory requirement level or for one reason or other the minimum requirement level itself has been raised, and when the top management attempts to design a system with higher efficiency. Whether the new system is designed originally by the management itself, or acquired by studying the systems in other organizations, or imported from another country, the top management will try to establish it "deliberately" supported by the power they command. In such a case, the managers will try to integrate the new system into the overall corporate system and furthermore attempt to formalize it vis-a-vis the members of the organization as a "management system". Category one is the case where the new scheme has not yet settled in among the members of the organization as their customary thought pattern. Even in such a case, it is often referred to as a "system". However, strictly speaking, it is still in the process of being systematized and thus has not been fully established as a system as such. In fact, it may still clash with the mentalities of the organization members and end up a mere shell or be discarded. Or, it may establish itself as a system only after going through considerable changes, in a form very different from what was originally conceived. In other words, it could be a part of what is included in the broader concept of a system. However, because there are many cases when it is already established in other societies, it might well be called a "system" in our discussion here.

(ii) The second category refers to those management systems that are adequately established within the individual companies but have not yet reached the point of spreading widely in the society. In this case, within the scope of that given organization at any rate, the management system has already been established among the members as their customary thought pattern and adequately serving as their working rule. It can be a system originating abroad, or it can be something that will strike roots only in that society.

(iii) Category three includes those management systems adopted by individual companies that have also struck roots widely in the society. In such cases, the management systems that were originally implemented by individual organizations often display a type of constraining force that might qualify them to be referred to as "social systems". For example, in a society like Japan's where the systems of liftetime employment and age-grade pay have become widespread and universal, even the top management, and of course the rank-and-file employees, find it difficult to take any action going against these systems.

That is to say, even if a member of an organization wanted to relocate to another institution, the possibility of doing so is extremely limited in Japan. Even if the companies also wished to abolish these systems, they will have to confront not only resistance within the company but also other circumstances such as the shortage of capable persons to assume middle-management posts brought about by the overall difficulties in mid-career recruitment. Another example is, if most of the companies decide to employ the method of recruiting new personnel once a year (which is the prevailing situation in Japan), a company would find it nearly impossible to go against the current. Due to this constraining force, it is not easy even for the top management to reform a system once this last stage of development has been reached, even though the system may have originally been developed very "deliberately" by the managers themselves. This also explains the Japanese phenomenon of stubborn resistance towards change or even a move to keep down changes in people's mentalities even when the management system has lost its rational basis or when the mentalities of the members involved are actually changing.

From this approach of looking at management from an institutional angle, the various factors that relate to the formation of management systems can be illustrated as shown in Figure 1.3.

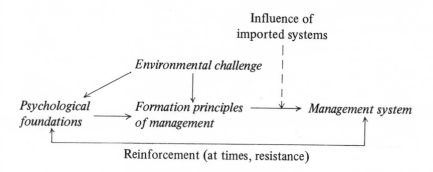

Figure 1.3

Chapter 2

PSYCHOLOGICAL FOUNDATIONS OF JAPANESE-STYLE MANAGEMENT

Once upon a time, I used to systematically seek the foundations of Japanese-style management in the group-oriented mentality of the Japanese people and to conduct analyses on various characteristic features of Japanese management from this viewpoint. Indeed, this angle of approach is a very effective means of explaining many of the various aspects of Japanese-style management. But it is also true that there are a number of other aspects to Japanese management that cannot be explained from this viewpoint.

This book will attempt to study the psychological foundations supporting Japanese-style management from a broader perspective. We will focus on three psychological traits of the Japanese people as well as the inter-relations between these three elements. The three psychological traits are: (1) the situational conformity of the Japanese; (2) the unique human bonds that I refer to as the "familiarity relationship," and the mutual moral expectations and trust accompanying such a relationship; and, (3) the type of group-orientation found among the Japanese. The situational conformity of the Japanese will be taken up first.

2.1 SITUATIONAL CONFORMITY
2.1.1 Westerners are Strict about Time

It has been pointed out often by many scholars and critics that the Japanese display a kind of flexibility in their activities. I myself, during my few years of study in the United States as well as through my dealings with Americans and Europeans more recently, have often witnessed an interesting contrast between the relative lack of "versatility" among Westerners and the flexible reactions of the Japanese. I shall, therefore, begin by introducing a rather personal experience with regard to this point.

We have been giving our oldest son "Royal Jelly" (a kind of nutritional supplement) every morning since shortly after he was born. Whether it is because of this or not I do not know, but my son is very healthy and has hardly ever come down with a cold. He also seems to be above average as concerns his physical growth. The instructions on the bottle of Royal Jelly say that since the jelly is affected easily by stomach acid it should be taken right after getting out of bed and that you shouldn't eat for thirty minutes after that. So, my son, who is not given anything to eat for thirty minutes when he is in fact quite hungry, would often ask his mother for breakfast. But the reply is always, "You have to wait for thirty minutes." Thus the phrase "thirty minutes" was among the first words the child learnt along with "mommy" and "daddy". One morning, he must have been exceptionally hungry. He was literally pleading with his mother for breakfast. I was quite surprised to hear the dialogue between my son and his mother. My wife, who is an American of Scottish origin, was saying to our son, "It's not thirty minutes yet. You have to wait *two* more minutes." Shortly often she said this, the timer rang cheerfully and my son got his breakfast.

As I said, this dialogue surprised me in no small way and I brought this up at a certain workshop consisting mainly of foreigners. Having heard my story, a German-American lady commented in fluent Japanese, "I would also make him wait two more minutes. At least we of the German race would do so." So it seems that this reaction was not something peculiar to the Scottish race! It was also interesting to see a *sansei* (third generation) Japanese-American lady get a bit excited and say to this lady, "For heaven's sake! It's not as if he was taking medicine!" Does this mean that even if you are of Japanese origin, by the time you reach the third generation you get so "Westernized" that if not for taking meals you do stick to your "two minutes" for medicine? After all, we are not talking about the use of clinical thermometers. Even with medicine, a Japanese who tries to observe the last two minutes would most probably be regarded as being slightly strange.

It is said that when you ask Japanese people working for Japanese companies stationed abroad what they think about Japanese-style management as compared to the European systems, many of them will comment that the local people (i.e. non-Japanese) do not put in much overtime. This again reflects the strict time-mindedness of the American and European people. Dr. Tadashi Mito, Professor at St. Paul's University in Tokyo, who introduced this story, comments as follows.

"You see so many people who wait with their handbags and brief cases on their desks or laps so that they can leave right on time.... Even if one is in the middle of a job, he or she leaves when the time comes. The fact that putting in a few more minutes would finish that job doesn't make any difference. Whether he is half way through a calculation, or half way through a letter, or even nine-tenths through the task, he stops and leaves. I even saw people leave in the middle of spelling out a word...." (*Ooyake to Watakushi* (The Public and I), Mirai-sha, p. 13)

If this is the case at the end of the day on a Friday, it wold certainly affect work efficiency greatly.

Such a difference between the Westerners and the Japanese is also reflected in their respective cooking customs. Recipes used by many Americans tend to be far more detailed than Japanese ones with regard to the amount of each ingredient and time. And, there seems to be a definite tendency among the Americans to cook as precisely as possible according to the directions in the recipe. They seem not to be too skilled in "playing with the amount in the spoon."

This kind of flexibility among the Japanese, especially noticeable when shown in contrast to the behavioural patterns of Americans and Europeans, seems to derive from various tendencies peculiar to the Japanese race, such as the reluctance of the Japanese to draw a clear line in processing matters, their situational conformity, i.e. the sharp perception of the "situation" and the unique sense of balance with reality, and the quick orientation and reaction to cope with various situations made possible by these mentalities. For a Japanese, there is absolutely nothing wrong with giving your child breakfast a few minutes before the thirty minutes are up if he or she is particularly hungry that morning. It is only natural for a Japanese to use discretion in deciding on the number of spoonfuls of ingredients to be used and making the dish slightly sweeter or saltier depending on preferences or the situation. This kind of situational conformity has perhaps even become one of the principles of life of the Japanese people. Moreover, this behavioural principle governs personal relations among the Japanese. In Japanese society, changes based on situational variations are tolerated to a considerable degree. A well-known Japanologist, Rabbi Marvin Tokayer, described this tendency of the Japanese very clearly in one of his books.

"In Japan, the word 'watashi' (meaning 'I') tends to be treated more like an object than a subject. 'I' is also a situation. . . . Situations always change and turn. Thus, 'I' also changes. 'I' cannot control such situational changes. Therefore, 'I' am not responsible. This is the basic idea. . . . When a Japanese person says 'I will do it,' the true implication of the statement is interpreted to mean 'I will do my utmost to accomplish it, provided that the situation allows me to.' Rephrased, this means that 'I' may not do it should the situation be unfavourable, because if the situation changes, I am not going to be able to do it. . . . " (M. Tokayer, *Nippon-jin wa Shinda* (Gone Are the Japanese), translated by Soichiro Hakozaki, pp. 78-9)

The situational conformity of the Japanese is also reflected in their concept of responsibility, of contracts, and the attitude towards rules and regulations. It is a common Japanese concept that rules and regulations that are applied to various situations should be done so with flexibility and that it is absurd to use them as an absolute yardstick. I am not certain about children or stubborn "thickheads" who never "grew up", but real "grown ups" at any rate will tend to think that way.

2.1.2 The Phrase "Yoroshiku" Makes Sense in Japanese Companies

Situational conformity as described in the foregoing section is extremely significant when working as a team. This is obvious and needs no further explanation than to ask the readers to think of how baseball, soccer, or other team sports are played. A competent team is one which can quickly register the opponent's positions, its own members' positions, and the ball's position in ever-changing circumstances and position its players in crucial spots at all times. It is apparent what will happen to the game if the players do not act in any other way than as indicated specifically by their managers and coaches. The Japanese, on the whole, are accustomed to act in a situational conformable manner in their daily behaviour and in carrying out their tasks. Needless to say, Americans and Europeans are theoretically capable of practising situational conformity as proven by their excellent soccer teams, for example. However, at least with regard to carrying out one's assignment or work in the company, they clearly lack situational conformity as compared with their Japanese counterparts. The following comment by Koji Kobayashi, Chairman of NEC (Nippon Electric Company), concerning this point is quite interesting. This is his view with regard to differences in the management styles between Japan and the United States.

"NEC has an office in Washington, D.C. There are about twelve staff members working there. If this were an entirely Japanese set-up, all that the manager would have to do when he wants to step out of the office for a while is to say 'yoroshiku tanomu'* and the twelve members of his staff would keep on working without him. There is no need for any written instructions. However, in our Washington office, only the manager is Japanese and all other staff members are Americans. Therefore, the phrase 'yoroshiku tanomu' doesn't mean anything to them. The manager cannot leave the office until he prepares job instructions for each member. Here is a clear difference between the two. The same thing can be said for the overall management of a company. In Japan, the corporate president does not have to spell out exactly 'do this' and 'do that.' On the basis of the so-called 'telepathic understanding,' all of the let's say 10,000 members of the company try to figure out ways to make better products at lower cost, to increase sales, etc. In the United States, I would imagine that if the president did not give specific orders, he would be harassed by his subordinates asking

---

* The literal meaning is roughly, "Do as you think fit."

'what am I supposed to do?' 'how should I do this?' etc., etc. . . . ." (*Nihon Keizai Shimbun,* (Japan Economic Jounal) May 21, 1978)

The same tendency is pointed out also by Tadashi Mito, by his statement following the forementioned quote.

What is important here is that the characteristic tendency of the Japanese as pointed out by Kobayashi is supported by the ability to conform to the situation, a trait that is commonly noticeable among the Japanese. In the office or factory, the Japanese worker, just like a soccer player, quickly reads the circumstances he is placed in, i.e. the surrounding situation, his colleagues' reactions, and his own situation, and tries to respond to the needs of the overall situation.

This is to say that in Japanese companies, without top management having to issue orders constantly, the "situations" themselves give orders and in this sense the managers' burden is sharply reduced. Therefore, the main functions of a manager in a Japanese company are to grasp the entirety and to go around checking matters as well as to motivate the workers in order to maintain work morale among the members of the organization. As a result, the following statement by Kobayashi makes very good sense.

"In the United States, half of the corporate presidents and chairman I know have died of heart attacks after retiring at the age of 65. This goes to show the great pressure they are under. In Japan, the top management places faith in the company's strength. . . ." (*Nihon Keizai Shimbun,* May 21, 1978)

It is none other than this "corporate strength" that gives Japanese organizations their vitality and infuses strength in the members who carry out their work accurately without having to give them specific orders each time. To the contrary, in American and European societies, in order for an organization to carry out its tasks without having to give specific orders each time, it is necessary to specify the individual jobs in writing beforehand. Therefore, the American-type structure where individual tasks serve as the basic unit of the whole mechanism can perhaps be interpreted as a child of necessity.

In this sense, the approach taken by Mito of trying to explain Japanese-style management from the angle of its unique decision-making mechanism is indeed very interesting. Mito points out that in American and European-type organizations, people work in individual rooms and the communication channels and the direction of flow are clearly defined whereas in Japanese organizations, people work together in a big room and communication networks resembling a fishing net are created. Also, "Whereas in the United States and Europe top management is at the center of the communication channels and serves as the central unit in the decision-making process, in a set-up like that of Japan where the communication channels exist in the form of a network, each individual creates his own communication system, albeit differing in scope, and will serve as the central figure in the decision-making process within that system." According to Mito, a body like a *sogo shosha* (trading company) which has favourably impressed most Westerners by its dynamic functionability, can operate only through the existence of such a communication system. This analysis is most probably correct.

We must not forget that the creation of such a decision-making mechanism and the efficiency of the system are supported by the "situational conformity" of the Japanese people. This question of the relationship between the situational conformity of the Japanese and Japanese-style management will be dealt with in detail in Chapter 3. Section 3.3, "Differences between American-European organizations and Japanese organizations" and Chapter 4, Section 4.1.3, "Dynamism Brought about by flexibility of organization."

So far an academic analysis of "situational conformity" that, as we have seen, brings about significant distinctions between how organizations are run, has not been conducted to any satisfactory degree.

Once upon a time, Shunji Kobayashi, Professor at Waseda University, came up with the concept of "eleventh-hour situationalism" and tried to explain the situational conformity of the Japanese with this idea. Kobayashi must be admired for his keen insight in having detected this Japanese trait before many others did. However, as the nomenclature implies, the concept introduced by Kobayashi was accompanied by a very strong value judgement from the beginning resulting in a rather localized and incomplete analysis. Kobayashi explains "eleventh-hour situationalism" as the behaviour pattern of resorting to adhoc actions to keep up with changes in the situation, not the act of adapting positively and through initiative to the situational changes. It brings about 'actions without principles' so to speak. Therefore, an eleventh-hour situationalist does not have the capability of coming out with an empirical formula for future actions even after having experienced a drastic situational change. He strives only to adapt to the given situations in front of him." (*Nihon no Keiei Kankyo* (Management Environment in Japan), Edited by Masao Uno, Chapter 5, p. 119)

It is evident that not much can be derived from any analysis of the situational conformity of the Japanese based on such a definition. You cannot go beyond finding a few examples that fit the concept and criticize Japanese-style organizational phenomena. Even if we did accept that this concept describes one of the aspects of situational conformity of the Japanese, it must be studied as a part of a whole, that is, it must be analyzed in a broader perspective, together with and in relation to other aspects of the issue. What we need is a conceptual framework which we can use to analytically clarify the situational conformity of the Japanese itself.

In this sense, the idea of "outside in" introduced by Eshun Hamaguchi, Assistant Professor at Osaka University, brings us one step closer to the core of the issue. Here, Hamaguchi takes the two concepts of "inside out" and "outside in," both technical terms used by aircraft pilots, the former referring to the manoeuvring of the plane regarding the aircraft itself as the coordinate axis while the latter considers the outside world as the coordinate axis. He claims that this idea is applicable not only to piloting skills but also to the two types of awareness that a person can have when dealing with others. He considers it also to be the two models of conformity to group standards, and attempts to apply this idea to human behaviour in general and more specifically to his study of Japanology. This can be regarded as an excellent angle. (Details on this appear in Chapter 5 of *"Nihon-rashiesa" no Sai-hakken* (Re-discovery of Japanese-ness), by Eshun Hamaguchi, published by Nihon Keizai Shimbun.)

Deeper analysis of how this "situational conformity" of the Japanese was created, what its features are, and how it affects Japanese organizations shall be saved for another occasion. Nevertheless, I would like to point out three concepts – closely related to each other but need to be distinguished as three separate elements for the sake of analysis – that are regarded as useful in analyzing the interplay between man and situation. These are: (1) situational conformity; (2) situational relativity; and (3) situational adaptability. It should be noted here that the word "situational adaptability is used in a specific context, as will be explained later on. This is important because a broader interpretation of the phrase would include both situational conformity and situational relativity.

"Situational conformity", as has been illustrated with a number of examples, refers to the sharp perception of ever-changing situations and the attitude or ability to conform to such situational changes. "Situational relativity" refers to the tendency to greatly change one's perception, thought patterns, attitudes, etc. in accordance with the given situation. The concept of *uchi* (meaning roughly "within" or "inside") and *soto* ("without or "outside") perceived by most Japanese can be interpreted as one form of expressing this tendency. The three categories of personal relations among the Japanese people which will be explained in the following section can also be regarded as a reflection of the situational relativity of the Japanese. "Situational adaptability" refers to the attitude or capability of suppressing one's desires and adapting to the given situation. The great degree of adaptability that the Japanese people display in the context of "familiarity" relations, which will be explained in the next section, and in relationships with the groups is a reflection of situational adaptability. Moreover, the

Japanese approach to decision-making and the unanimous agreement system are also closely connected with this question of situational adaptability.

Situational relativity and situational adaptability will be dealt with more elaborately in the following discussion of Japanese-style personal relations and the group-oriented mentality of the Japanese.

2.2 TRUST RELATIONS WITHIN THE WORLD OF "FAMILIARITY"

2.2.1 Three Categories of Personal Relations

"While the Japanese attach value to behaviour and actions based on situational relativity, the Americans tend to take 'normative' actions based on certain public value concepts or group standards (a set of value concepts standardized by the group) regardless of the situation they find themselves in," comments Eshun Hamaguchi. (*Nihon-rashisa no Sai-hakken*, p. 15) Such "situational relativity" – oriented attitudes of the Japanese seem to be clearly reflected in Japanese-style personal relations. The Japanese behavioural pattern of drastically changing one's attitude depending on one's relationship with the other party brings out a characteristic feature that cannot be explained merely as a "question of degree". The great differences in the attitudes are, as is often pointed out, recognized in the great number of personal pronouns in the Japanese language, in the variety of honorific, polite, and demeaning expressions in the language, and the distinction of the two concepts of *uchi* (inside) and *soto* (outside).

When observing personal relations among the Japanese, you notice great differences depending on the degree of intimacy. Takeo Doi focuses on the existence (or non-existence) of self-restraint as being one of the criteria for the Japanese to distinguish their personal relations with others as being either *uchi* or *soto*. He explains as follows.

"Family members and relatives with whom you do not, relatively speaking, practice self-restraint, belong to your inside (*uchi*) group. However, people with whom you practise self-restraint and create a relationship of obligations is considered as the outside (*soto*) party. But there are cases where people regard acquaintances and people with obligatory relations as also being *uchi* and consider the world of total strangers, with whom you need not practise any self-restraint, as *soto*. At any rate, the line distinguishing *uchi* and *soto* is the question of whether self-restraint is at work or not in the relationship. . . ." (*Amae no Kozo*, p.38. Also published in English under the title *The Anatomy of Dependence*)*

---

* The paragraph quoted here has been taken directly from the original Japanese version and translated into English by the translator of the present book. It, therefore, differs somewhat in style from the same passage in the English version of the quoted literature.

Since I attach importance to the group affiliation awareness of the Japanese and also find significance in the tendency whereby the concepts of *uchi* and *soto* are formed around one's affiliated group, I have a slightly different idea about *uchi* and *soto* from Doi's, which, he says is centred around the idea of self-restraint.*

Nevertheless, Doi's classification of Japanese-style personal relationships is very useful. I categorize personal relations among the Japanese according to the type of "moral expectations" and the pattern of reaction thereto, of which self-restraint is probably a part. The scope of this categorization seems to correspond more or less to Doi's three-way classification. The three categories I define for personal relations among the Japanese are: (1) the "unconnected" relationship; (2) the "familiarity" relationship; and, (3) the "unconstrained" relationship.

(i) The "Unconnected" Relationship

This type of relationship is seen in passing relations, a typical example being between people passing each other in trains and stations. The Japanese cope with such encounters with a kind of indifference, not with "distrust" which is a more typical reaction in Western societies. Of course, there are cases when one builds interest in the other party, as in the case of being "attracted" to a person with an interesting costume and appearance or a charming lady. But that expresses more of an interest towards an "object" and not a personal or human interest towards the other like feelings of distrust or consideration. The fact that there are very few people in Japan who show some sort of thoughtfulness in a crowded train towards the elderly, pregnant women, or mothers with babies in their arms must be a reflection of such a mentality.

The basic factor that characterizes such human relations is the lack — or extreme paucity — of mutual moral expectations. That is the reason why Japanese people can act without any self-restraint in such circumstances. It is also a fact that in this type of a relationship, you are never betrayed.

---

* The concepts of *uchi* and *soto* which were created around the existence of groups with objective structures have been forced to adapt to complex situations due to the increasing complexity of organizational structures and the tendency towards multi-structurization of groups. In other words, the concepts of *uchi* and *soto* determined by one's "affiliation" with a certain group have been pushed in the direction of selecting the group to conform to in accordance with constantly changing circumstances, and this has been brought about by the multi-structurization of groups. This can be regarded as an example of how the situational relativity of the Japanese people came to require the support of situational conformity. Details of this can be found in Chapter 4, Section I, of my previous book, *Nihon-teki Keiei no Hensei Genri.*

Since you vest no expectations to begin with, you will never be betrayed. This is why there are hardly any train passengers who warn or criticize a person to his face, or even express displeasure should that person throw his cigarette butt on the floor or push his way through to grab a seat in front of other people. They never had any more expectations to begin with.

In this relationship, the awareness of "shame" as described by Ruth Benedict is extremely weak and the principle of Hamaguchi's "outside in" is not at work either. Here, one's advocacy of his individuality lay totally exposed. There is a strong school of thought that there is no such thing as "individuality" among the Japanese. This, however, is not true. The question is what that "individuality" consists of and how it is expressed. It is quite misleading to claim that "Japanese don't have any individuality". It is not as if people always take shameless actions in such a relationship but are often nonchalant enough to take imprudent and vulgar actions. What serves as a brake against such vulgar behaviour going too far is perhaps the fear of having this boorish behaviour known to circles of "familiarity", e.g. the chance of there being someone who knows you among the crowd. The description of this next type of relationship follows.

(ii) The "Familiarity" Relationship

Once two Japanese know each other's names, social or professional status, and a bit of their personality, their relationship takes a completely new turn. In this type of a relationship, a certain kind of moral expectation is mutually created or expanded. Under this relationship, the awareness of "shame" is strongly felt by both parties and the principle of Hamaguchi's "outside in" is at work. And, a "relationship with self-restraint" as described by Takeo Doi is established. At the same time that moral expectations are created, a feeling of trust is vested in the other party, i.e. the faith that the other person will not betray your expectations. So, when this moral expectation, which is tacitly recognized widely among the members of the society or the group, is betrayed, the typically Japanese question of "moral responsibility" is raised.

In the process of analyzing the Japanese concept of responsibility, I had great difficulties in comprehending this idea of "moral responsibility," something that plays a highly crucial role in Japanese society yet is so hard to define. Recently, I have come to adopt the approach of trying to understand this subject in connection with the characteristic features of human relations among the Japanese. Indeed, it is this "moral responsibility" that is the essential concept of responsibility among the Japanese. And, the concept of moral responsibility, which is strongly characterized by the group-oriented mentality of the Japanese people, forms the core of the modern Japanese idea of responsibility.

That the question of moral responsibility arises when moral expectations are betrayed in a "familiarity" relationship is supported by the following fact. This "moral responsibility" is felt neither in the forementioned "unconnected" relationship nor in the "unconstrained" relationship described later. Even when the idea of responsibility does exist in these other relationships, it is "responsibility" in the legal sense – in the Japanese context of "legal" – and not in the sense of moral responsibility.

The "familiarity" relations among the Japanese show a number of characteristic features. First of all, once the relationship is established there is a tendency to continue until it is broken by a dispute. Even if the two parties are physically separated for one reason or another, the relationship is easily revived by a re-union. Secondly, in this type of a relationship, the maintenance of mutual good will is stressed and thus harmonious and conformable relations are sought. Mutual good will is sought even if it means paying the price of restraining one's own desires. And it is the need for expressing this mutual good will that brings about the customs of summer gift giving (*chugen*), year-end gift giving (*seibo*), bringing gifts on every visit, the massive exchange of new year's cards, etc. All of these semi-compulsory customs continue strongly to date in Japan. Thirdly, in a "familiarity" relationship, there is a strong tendency to value the order of things that one has grown accustomed to and thus strongly resist any changes in the order, especially the status order.

As the recently popular term "crab society" connotes, it is often pointed out that in the Japanese society there is a lot of "leg pulling" of those who try to climb the social ladder. This seems to reflect the tendencies we have so far studied in a "familiarity" relationship. As human relations within communities became more and more detached due to the rapid urbanization of the post-war era, it seemed that this tendency was rapidly disappearing from communal societies. On the other hand, there appeared strong tendencies to avoid drastic changes in the status order within schools, companies, and other occupational societies.

(iii) The "Unconstrained" Relationship

As intimacy increases between two Japanese, their relationship takes another turn. In this new stage of the relationship, the mutual good will has developed into such a solid thing that neither needs to make any special effort at maintaining it and they can still count on each other's good will and favour. It is assumed that the good will cannot be hurt by verbal attacks or a temporary misunderstanding. It is also mutually assumed that they will be forgiven even if they push a bit hard and they are allowed to confess things of a personal nature. In this relationship, the expectation towards the other party grows even greater than a moral one. But even when one party betrays the expectation, he is forgiven as long as he can prove that there were no ill intentions. This concept is close to what Takeo Doi called "close acquaintances with whom you do not have to exercise self-restraint," but covers a broader scope than what one would call "close acquaintances" such as friends and colleagues.

2.2.2 Familiarity Relationship in Business

This kind of Japanese-style human relations is also brought into the world of business where one would tend to think that the whole network of relations would be built more on "dry" calculations. The concept of familiarity affects the style of doing business to a great extent. Whereas in American and European companies, "business is conducted on the basis of cool calculations supported by careful credit analysis and rational 'insurance systems,'," (Kohei Hisaeda, *Keiyaku no Shakai, Mokuyaku no Shakai* (Contractual Society, Taçit-Agreement Society)), in Japan the start of business is often marked by the establishment of a "familiarity" relationship. A number of examples will be introduced here to illustrate Japanese-style human relations in business.

Case Example 1: The story goes back as many as twenty years. There was a salesman of a small sporting goods shop. This man had just graduated from high school and was still a beginner salesman in his twenties. One day, he got on his motorcycle and started passing through the university where I taught, just dropping in here and there and spreading cheerful 'hellos'. Those who remember him from those days say that he hardly gave the impression of having come on sales calls.

In the beginning, he frequented the physical education faculty room and engaged in very simple conversations like "How are you?" or "How are things going these days?" But he never talked business and always left after a few minutes. Roughly half a year passed like this. During this time, the physical education faculty regarded him as an "odd fellow" but also started building an intimate feeling towards him. Soon, the teachers started placing orders with the young salesman for inexpensive articles with small profit margins, such as detonators for pistols used in track events. Whenever the school needed something urgently, and the teachers asked him "Does your shop carry such-and-such?" the young man would answer "Yes we do!" With the big manufacturers the school often had to wait a full week for delivery of goods. But with him, when they told him "We need such-and-such by tomorrow," he would reply "Yes, sir!" and the goods would be there the next day. If they insisted, he would even bring the goods on the same day. The school kept on purchasing commercially profitable items such as balls from another place, but from time to time began acquiring cheap and heavy items such as lime powder or urgently needed articles from him. The salesman never complained and kept on supplying the goods he was told to bring.

As this relationship continued, the salesman and the school people became quite intimate so that they could talk to each other freely, and he was soon participating in the conversations among the teachers.

In the physical education faculty room, there was a teacher who was very fond of playing Japanese chess. The salesman now and then went over and studied the board on which a game was being played. Roughly a year after the salesman started dropping in, someone asked him, "Can you play Japanese chess?" He replied, "Yes, I can." So now he was even playing Japanese chess with the teachers and stayed on for an hour or so when he dropped in at lunch time. And, with time, the school started placing orders with him also for commercially profitable articles such as balls. Three years after his first appearance at school all of the necessary sporting goods were being purchased from him.

Some ten years later, the same salesman became independent and started running his own shop. By this time, the school was placing major orders with him, sometimes running into millions of yen. Other sections within the school also relied on him to bring even non-sporting goods such as armbands.

When teachers made personal purchases from him, it is said that he never asked for the money on the spot. It was only when the teacher asked him, "Isn't it about time I pay you? How much do my bills add up to so far?" then he would say "Let me check it," go back, and bring the invoice on his next visit. There, he would present the invoice and say, "You can pay whenever you wish. This is what the figures add up to." Twenty years have gone by since his first visit to the school. Recently, he dropped in at the school and asked one of the teachers. "Sir, I am thinking of buying a house. Can you act as guarantor for my bank housing loan?" The teacher concerned agreed to this right off. The relationship between the two had gone beyond that of a salesman and client, and developed into a close friendship.

Case Example 2: I recently came across a story that depicts quite a different situation from the first example. But, depending on how you look at it, it could be interpreted as being rather similar in some ways. Dr. Yutaka Osawa of Osaka University told me the story. According to him, a textile factory in Niigata was eager to do business with one of the leading wholesalers in Osaka in order to expand its distribution network. The wholesaler, however, was not the kind of an establishment that would readily start business with a stranger. The manufacturer sent one of its officers to Osaka, some 600 km from Niigata. However, when this officer went to the wholesaler and asked for a meeting with the president, he only got a brush off. But the officer did not give up and started frequenting the wholesaler. He would just drop in now and then, tell jokes to the female employees, sip tea, and go back. This sort of visit was repeated over a period of half a year. Eventually, the president of the wholesaler said, "Hmm, an interesting fellow. Maybe I should see him once." Even since, the president did meet with this officer now and then but was not yet ready to nod his head to a business deal with the manufacturer. By the time another half year had passed, a kind of intimacy developed between the two men. So, after one year, the manufacturer succeeded in clinching a deal with this wholesaler. Once the business relationship was established, mutual feelings of trust expanded rapidly and they even got to the point of doing business over the phone.

Upon receipt of a cable from the wholesaler, the factory would without hesitation ship the products as per the order. Payment was always made on time and by now the trust relationship between the two parties has grown extremely solid.

Case Example 3: Once, I observed the activities of an insurance solicitor by accompanying a very capable life insurance saleswoman for half a day. I was very impressed when I saw her conclude a life insurance contract for a rather high value with a client right in my presence. The secrets of selling life insurance told by the lady were very interesting in the context of Japanese-style human relations. Many insurance salespeople depend largely on personal introductions through relatives, friends, and acquaintances, and would not think twice about travelling great distances when such an introduction is obtained. But this saleswoman said that she did not do such inefficient things.

As far as she was concerned, if you travel to far away cities like Kyoto and Kobe and end up with no contract, it would mean a loss of time. She says that it is better to exert more efforts at establishing good human relations with the people in *your* "territory". Surprisingly enough, what she considers to be her territory is a mere block in the office district of northern Osaka within which there are several office buildings. She spends her whole day, morning and afternoon, in this one district and frequents the various sections and departments of many companies. According to her, the name of the game is to frequently show up for very short visits each time.

And, when she visits an office, her movement pattern is cleverly designed. She makes sure that her presence is being noticed by all the workers in the room. If she goes around from one desk to the neighbouring desk as shown in Fig. 2.1(a), the visit would be over in no time at all. Instead, she would decide on a "starting point" and from there visit a desk or two, exchange a few words, and then come back to her starting position. (See Fig. 2.1-(b)) She would look around the whole office from her position and then resume her second round of visits to some of the other desks.

Those people she could not say hello to in the morning, she would come back for after lunch or later in the afternoon. In this way, a few years after starting her sales activities, the lady became acquainted with the faces of most of the office workers in the district. And with many of them, she became close. She has even acted as matchmaker for many of them, and she would also feed them information on good buys around town. If one of them tells her that his wife has started making something to earn pocket money, she would help sell these "masterpieces". The relationship has gone beyond that of an insurance saleswoman and clientele. She has become a kind and merry "auntie" for them. So, this widow who was once at a loss when her husband died and left her with children to look after, has recently renovated her house, was commended by the company for her performance, and says she is very happy.

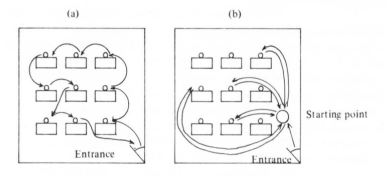

Figure 2.1

2.2.3 Factors Bringing about Familiarity

Since within an "unconnected" relationship mutual moral expectations do not exist and there is very little awareness of moral responsibility, it is only natural in the world of business that you should be suspicious of someone with whom you only have an "unconnected relationship". In fact, since there are many interests involved for both parties, such feelings of suspicion are liable to appear more strongly. So, when doing business in Japan, it is very important to establish "familiarity" relations and constantly expand their scope. However, it is not easy to create a "familiarity" relationship in the world of business since concrete interests are involved. Usually, it takes far greater time and effort than if you were trying to establish a "familiarity" relationship in your private life. The following factors can be regarded as necessary for creating the familiarity relationship.

(i)   That the frequency and duration of contact is ample.

(ii) That the contact is personal.

(iii) That, if possible, a common experience is shared.

(iv) That the habits and nature of the other party is mutually known to some extent.

(v)   That some feeling of security and good will is created.

(i)   Significance of Frequency of Contacts

For us to "familiarize" ourselves with an automobile or a sophisticated piece of machinery we have purchased, it is necessary to operate it for a certain period of time at a certain frequency. It goes without saying that such a pattern is far more effective in terms of "familiarization" than if we have operated it for the same total number of hours but continuously at one time. This idea holds true, to a large extent, for the establishment of human relations as well.

In particular, in the process of two Japanese shifting from a totally unknown and indifferent relationship to a close relationship, the frequency of personal contacts seems to have an important bearing. In the first example given, although the initial contacts consisted of short visits with an exchange of only a few words, the fact that the salesman frequented the school helped to create a kind of intimacy between the two parties before they knew it. In the second example, although the corporate officer from the manufacturer did not see the president of the wholesaler in person, by dropping into the wholesaler's office now and then he succeeded in making the president say "what an interesting fellow" and built a feeling of intimacy towards him. It can be assumed that stories about him had reached the president on a number of occasions via the female employees.

The university where I teach is a rather small school where seminar style classes are held rather than lecture style classes. The teaching staff and the students are on relatively close terms and compared to the big universities the relationship between the two can be regarded as good. Whether it is for this reason or not I cannot really say, but there has been little student trouble and as far as I know there has never been anyone arrested by the police for a serious offense.

Nevertheless, since each of these seminars is held only once a week, it competes very poorly with club activities and language classes where the frequency of contacts is greater. The students tend to form groups not around the seminar units but around their language classes and most of them end up finding close friends among the people from the same language class, not from the same seminar. There are also many students who put priority on club activities rather than on seminars. It is not uncommon for a student to come to me and ask, without any hesitation, that his turn at making a presentation to the seminar be delayed because he is too busy with his club activities. These facts clearly illustrate the importance of frequency of mutual contacts in establishing close relations in Japanese society.

(ii) Importance of Period of Contacts

The three case examples also illustrate the importance of the period of contacts. That is not to say that contacts lasting many hours each are important, but that even if the duration of each contact is short, you need to let a certain period of time elapse after your initial contact. It is interesting to note that in all three cases, roughly six months were required to create the first springboard. Of course, in the formation of a personal friendship, you often see a very quick development of intimacy. But in business transactions where concrete interests are involved this sort of time and period is usually necessary.

(iii) Creation of Good Will and Expansion of Trust

In the first case example, by willingly accepting even a very small order, the salesman succeeded in gradually obtaining the good will of the customers. In those days, the teachers are said to have looked on the salesman as an "odd fellow." With this kind of good will as the foundation, he began participating in their conversations, even joining in their chess games, and managed to promote intimacy. Furthermore, by indicating his feeling of trust towards the teachers by never pushing for payment, he won trust for himself in return. He even created a trust relationship so strong that he was able to obtain from one of the clients a commitment as guarantor for a housing loan, a role that even close relatives hesitate to accept nowadays.

Such a feeling of trust is something that is created by showing one's faith and earnestness over a long period of time. It is a very strong tie, but can be destroyed in no time once the trust is betrayed. Therefore in human relations like this, you must never betray the trust. The fact that in the second example, business could be carried out on the basis of a telephone call signifies that the relationship is supported by a strong sense of mutual trust.

(iv) Importance of all-around Contacts

The top saleswoman introduced in the third example succeeded in establishing close relations with her potential clients. She makes efforts to maintain every possible kind of contacts, from locating goods that her clients are looking for to matchmaking for young couples. It is even said that some of her office worker clients occasionally came up with a profitable deal through her good offices.

In the two other examples as well, intimacy is enhanced by avoiding business matters in the beginning and just engaging in small talk, exchanging jokes, and joining in games. Thus, it seems that the development of an all-around contact is quite important in establishing good human relations in Japanese society. In school life, too, we often note tht the intimacy between teacher and students is strengthened sharply when the teacher does not confine himself to academic activities but goes out and participates in the students' softball games and marathon events. I myself have experienced a rapid development of intimacy with students just on the basis of several matches of arm wrestling.

As these examples show, the contacts necessary to create a "familiarity" relationship must include some personal elements. Even if we received a greeting card in printed form every six months from a local politician whom we do not know, we would most likely glance at it and throw it away. If instead we received a hand-written letter every now and then from a local politican we know of, our attitude would be quite different.

The same tendency cannot be ignored in the business world. The more occasions you have to go out on the golf course together, the easier it is to establish a "familiarity" relationship. Since it is much easier to create a "familiarity" relationship in the context of one's private life than to try to do so in the world of business, contacts made outside of business are often used to help create and maintain a "familiarity" relationship in business. In the first two examples, during the initial stage, neither the salesman nor the corporate officer even mentioned business but engaged in talk about the weather and other petty things, and left, only to come back some time later. Although it is difficult to determine exactly what their true intentions were, it certainly did serve an important function in assisting in the creation of a "familiarity" relationship.

This sort of unique features in human relations naturally affects the style of Japanese management in various ways. The three examples mentioned prove the importance of such human relations in the field of sales. The same kind of relationship also characterizes bank-client relations and supervisor-worker relations. Japanese-style personnel recruitment, personnel management, in-house training, and motivation management of the employees are certainly not detached from such human relations.

I would like to add one more comment on this point, namely regarding names of well-known companies and the "familiarity" relationship. Just as many popular TV stars have created a "one-way familiarity relationship" with the viewers, well-known major companies have also established a "one-way familiarity relationship", supported by the company's credibility, with the people. Thus, in Japanese society, products made by well-known major companies are referred to as *"mehkah-hin"* (meaning "maker's goods" or "brand goods") with which the consumers have developed a type of intimacy and have vested their confidence.

As can be seen, since in Japanese society the "familiarity" relationship plays a crucial role in the business world as well, Japanese companies when doing business do so anticipating a long-term relationship. They place more stress on the creation and maintenance of good will and mutual trust with the other party rather than on short-term interests. This forces them to make efforts at coordinating mutual interests and display a keen sense of long-term balance. Just as the establishment of a "familiarity" relationship in the business world is far more difficult than in the world of everyday life, because of the concrete interests involved, so is maintaining it. The "familiarity" relationship in business is always exposed to the danger of being easily destroyed. And, once it is destroyed, putting it back together is extremely difficult, if not impossible. Realizing this, Japanese companies show various marks of consideration and make many efforts to maintain a mutual "familiarity" relationship, one of the most important kinds of trust relations.

2.3 GROUP-ORIENTED MENTALITY
2.3.1 Groupism and Group-orientation

I have made studies on the psychological foundations of Japanese-style management approaching it mainly from the angle of the group-orientation of the Japanese and analyzing the relationship between the features of Japanese-style management and their psychological foundations. First, it is necessary to clarify the relationship between groupism and group-orientation.

Hiroshi Hazama, who studied Japanese-style management from the angle of "groupism", describes the term as follows.

"Groupism is the philosophy of group-centredness (priority-on-group), i.e. the idea of placing priority on the interest of the group before that of the individual in an individual-group relationship. Or, it is a moral ideology of regarding it as 'desirable' or 'virtuous' to do so. . . . In fact, it can be said that the very idea of setting the individual against the group is an attitude based on the philosophy of individualism. Under the concept of groupism, the most 'desirable' form of relationship between the individual and the group is not for them to oppose each other but for the two to become one. . . . Individual (interests) equals group (interests) and group (interests) equals individual (interests). According to such a school of thought, the attitude of 'for the company' which may appear as being self-sacrificial to outsiders is, in fact, not a sacrifice for others but an act for one's own good as far as that individual is concerned. . . ." (*Nihon-teki Keiei: Shudanshugi no Kozai* (Japanese-Style Management: Merits and

Demerits of Groupism), Nikkei Shinsho, p. 16)

This description no doubt offers a very significant clue for grasping the characteristics of Japanese-style management. But the term "group orientation" reflects the unique mentality, that is clearly recognizable among the Japanese, that supports or is at the root of a concept or ideology. Thus, what I want to emphasize is not merely the question of "interests" but rather the manner in which the Japanese perceive and feel things, something that involves delving into the deep rooted psychology of the Japanese, seeking something so deeply embedded that it even governs the emotions of the Japanese. This manner of perception is reflected vividly in the way a Japanese looks at his relationship with others, his relationship with various groups and society, and in his concern towards these parties. As a result, in terms of organizational features, it also dictates the Japanese concept of responsibility and status awareness. I believe that "groupism" as described by Hazama can exist only when you accept the existence of such "group orientation" among the Japanese.

It is perhaps significant to make a few observations on the relations between ideology and psychology. I believe that the two mutually regulate each other. The basic direction of this regulatory force, however, is assumed to be psychology → ideology. This is clear when one recalls what eventually happened to the ideology of European-style individualism that countless "intellectuals" tried to introduce into Japan after the Meiji Period and to the ideology of "democracy" that was propagated on such a grand scale after the Second World War. Or, one simply needs to think about the case when Japanese companies try to implement Japanese-style management, as it is, in the United States, or Europe, or the Middle East. In other words, an ideology is built upon a certain psychological foundation and can function effectively only when it is accepted and supported by the national psychology of the people in that society. Therefore, groupism can function because it is being supported by the deep-rooted group-orientation of the Japanese and on this foundation it derives such features as the group structure of Japanese companies and intra-group and inter-group competition.

2.3.2 Participation and Affiliation

The group-orientation of the Japanese, as has been explained so far, strongly characterizes the perception of the relationship between oneself and others as well as of one's position in the "world". It is said that man is a "social animal". In that we desire to relate ourselves to others and become part of a group, there are no basic differences between the Japanese and the Americans or Europeans.

However, because of the difference in how one copes with the tension existing between an individual and the group, a substantial difference is recognized in the individual-group relationship bteween the Japanese and Westerners. With Americans and Europeans who try to minimize the tension by limiting their relationship with a group both functionally and time-wise, and by securing the freedom to leave the group, there is a tendency to avoid being too involved in one particular group. This is accomplished by participating in many groups. As Vance Packard points out in his work *The Pyramid Climbers,* the corporate executives who happen to find themselves deeply involved with the company often show painful reactions towards the situation. To the contrary, a Japanese will cope with the tension existing between the individual and the group by distinguishing between *tatemae* (official stance) and *honne* (true intentions). Therefore, the tension is absorbed into the individual psychology and as a result the Japanese are freed from coping with this in any realistic sense as would be required of Westerners.

Consequently, a Japanese would get deeper and deeper involved in a certain group, to the extent of identifying himself within the society as a member of that group and, at the same time, as will be explained in Chapter 4, still keep his dissatisfactions concerning the group and unfulfilled desires to himself. Under the pressure of the lifetime employment system, the dissatisfactions will even turn inward to the extent of creating nihilistic impulses among the group members. Therefore, the idea of "fusion" and "integration" of the individual and the whole may exist as a theory, but cannot be regarded as a true description of the realities of Japanese-style management.

Whereas a Westerner's relationship with the group may be termed appropriately as "participating", that of a Japanese is more precisely "affiliation". In this case, "affiliation" means that you are identifying yourself in the society (or within a certain world) as a member of a given group. This practice of identification is clearly illustrated in the way one introduces oneself to a stranger.

For example, an American, or a European, or even an Arab or an Indian for that matter, ordinarily states his name first and then adds the necessary explanation regarding himself. Among the friendly American students, there are even those who just state their first name, like "John" or "Bob" and shake your hand. To the contrary, aside from cases when you have no particular "affiliation" to speak of or it is absolutely unnecessary, like living in the same neighbourhood, you usually state your affiliation, followed by your name, such as *"Musashi Daigaku no Iwata desu"* (meaning "I am Musashi University's Iwata). In particular, this is considered to be the most convenient practice over the phone when you cannot see the other party's face. In an extreme example, there are cases when you only get the name of the group the other person is affiliated with.

Again, I draw upon a personal experience, but an interesting one, concerning this difference between the reactions of an American and a Japanese. It seems that my students and colleagues who telephone me at my residence get a slight "shock" when they hear the voice of a woman responding in Japanese with an American accent. Teachers who have lived abroad seem to be puzzled for a moment as to whether to speak in English or in Japanese and mutter in English, "This is Jiro Asaba speaking." Teachers with whom I am on close terms usually state their names. Those teachers I do not know too well and the students generally say "I am Musashi University's such-and-such."

Interestingly enough, most of the school's administrative staff only state the section or office name like, "This is the economics department office." So my wife thinks, "Hmm. A section can't place a call. It is a human being's voice, so he must have a name." Thus, with her newly acquired skill of the language she asks, "Who is this speaking please?" Despite the fact that she asked *who* it was, the party on the line thinks that she did not quite get what he said and repeats, "this is the economics department office." For my American wife, a call in which the party does not identify himself is a sign of someone playing a joke on her. So, she raises her voice higher and asks again, "Who is this!" The other party does not give up, "This is the EC-O-NOM-ICS DE-PART-MENT OF-FICE!" Afterwards, she complains to her Japanese husband, "Japanese are devious. Many of them don't even tell you who they are when they call." This is probably a trick played by the differences in the concept of affiliation.

In Japanese society where a person is identified in accordance with his affiliation with a group, the question of whether a person is the *uchi* ("inside") man of the group or *soto* ("outside") man of the group becomes an important element in evaluating each other. Also, it brings about the unique Japanese mentality of being strongly concerned with matters regarding the group you are affiliated with and being quite indifferent to the world outside the group. Consequently, features such as treasuring the good will of your colleagues and your evaluation within the group, the unique sense of responsibility that is strongly directed towards the group, and the specific Japanese concept of status (as will be described in Chapter 3) are very commonly recognized.

2.3.3 Three-layer Structure of Human Relations and Group Affiliation

The forementioned three categories of human relations among the Japanese can be represented as three concentric circles (as shown in Figure 2.2), with the individual in the center and each circle representing the degree of intimacy. Needless to say, this is a very rough illustration of the relationships. How these three concentric circles will look depends on the nature of that particular individual as well as on what type of friendship he enjoys. There may be cases, as with a bigoted researcher or an artist, where the range of "familiarity" relations is relatively narrow but his range of "unconstrained" relationships is vast. A capable businessman or salesman may have a wide range of people with whom he enjoys "familiar" relations but a limited range of "unconstrained" relationships. There are cases where the "familiarity" relations are concentrated mainly around his residential community, as in the case of many small shop owners, for example. On the other hand, the employee of a big company living in a large housing complex may find his "familiarity" relationships concentrated around human relations within the office.

Figure 2.2

Now, when a person is about to "affiliate" himself with a certain group, especially with an occupation-related group, the new affiliation awareness will force the three-layered structure of his human relations to undergo some alterations. In one's occupational group (i.e. most commonly the company or organization one works for), "familiarity" relations are rapidly established by frequent contacts, sharing of experiences, and various business policies that promote "familiarity" relationships. At the same time these intra-group "familiarity" relations that have been created through affiliation awareness seem to create a kind of moral expectation that is somewhat different in nature from the moral expectations that exist in relations with business clients, for example. This is clear when we compare the so-called "moral responsibility" that comes to the fore when moral expectations outside of the group or between groups are betrayed to the responsibility towards the group that one has to assume when having betrayed expectations within the group.

When the group with which a person is affiliated is relatively small, the group will only represent a small part of his "unconstrained" and "familiarity" relationships. As shown in Figure 2-3-(a), his "familiarity" relations outside of the group will represent a larger share than that within the group. Reflecting such a phenomenon, in small and medium-sized companies, although close mutual relations exist, the group awareness tends to be weak. And, in such a case, it is assumed that communal human relations and occupational human relations are both complementary and competitive against each other. Moreover, because of this, the smaller a company is the greater the tendency for it to be merely a business enterprise while its function as a going concern becomes less recognizable.

As the size of the company grows larger, the situation changes. A mammoth company will "engulf" a major portion of its members' "familiarity" relationships as illustrated in Figure 2-3-(b). For most of the members working for the company, the people they come in contact with day in and day out are their colleagues, and it is with these people that they share the experiences of parties and trips. As a result, their "familiarity" relationship is concentrated around human relations within the group, in this case, the company. Having lived in such an environment for some years, the occupational group becomes, for most people, a microcosm that defines their awareness and interests.

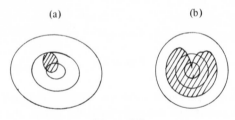

Figure 2.3

I would like to introduce an experience I myself had in this connection. After having graduated from a university in Tokyo, my new job sent me to Osaka. It turned out that there were only two other people from the same school dormitory who were going to move to Osaka. So, the three of us, after having bid farewell to our friends staying on in Tokyo, decided among ourselves that we would get together once a week, or at least twice a month, in Osaka.

However, once each of us started our new life with different companies in Osaka, began living with new colleagues in a fine company dormitory, became friends with many people from various schools in the dormitory, and gradually established our own close relationships with colleagues and seniors in the corporate department, the company started becoming a "world" for us. It was the office buddies I hurried through breakfast with at the dormitory canteen, with whom I ran to the train station together, then took lunch at the same table, and had a drink after work. Living in the dormitory, I was still with my company colleagues even after returning "home". The people I played tennis with at the company court on Saturday were company colleagues. The people I went hiking with on Sunday were also my company colleagues. For someone like myself in particular who had very little contact with the outside world because of the nature of my work, the people I negotiated with, the people I discussed with, the people I chatted with while rushing up the stairs, were all company colleagues. Being immersed in a lifestyle like this, it is surprising to note that even your interest in girls ends up being limited to the small world of your company. Consequently, the three boys who promised to meet once a week only got together on one occasion during my three years' stay in Osaka. Even this one exception was during a rally of the unions held in Tokyo, and two of the three who were representing different unions, just happened to come across each other during the rally.

After having lived in this microcosm for three years, I was relocated to a branch office in a local town. Feeling very sorry about leaving behind the human relations I had established around the fine head office building over a period of three years, I was walking through the streets of the local town dragging my heavy suitcase with me. When I stood in front of the small and rather scruffy pencil-shaped building in which the branch office rented some space, I had a weird psychological experience. For the first time, I realized that the "world" which had been my microcosm was merely one small company, one small organization, and that there was a big "world" existing outside the company. Telling it to the readers like this some years later, this may just sound like a commonplace story. But at the time, it was such an overwhelming experience for me that it almost made me feel dizzy.

This experience of mine within the microcosm and the experience of its collapse were very valuable for me in that they formed the starting point of my ideas when I began studying "Japanese management" some ten years later.

Human relations within the occupational group, especially in a gigantic company, help to further reinforce the group mentality of the Japanese. And the fact that such human relations are founded on the "familiarity" relationship brings about a tendency that here, too, long-term, stable relations are preferred as well as harmonious and conformable ones.

The psychological traits that we studied in this chapter are clearly reflected in the style of Japanese management. As I pointed out in the previous chapter, at the same time that Japanese-style management has undergone vast changes over the years in response to various environmental challenges, it has been built on a psychological foundation that supports and guides it towards a given orientation. In Chapter 3, the structure and mechanism of Japanese-style management supported by such psychological foundations will be discussed.

Chapter 3

STRUCTURE AND MECHANISM
OF JAPANESE MANAGEMENT

3.1 A PREREQUISITE

Over recent years, I have been encountering a very interesting phenomenon with regard to the employment situation of university graduates. At the university where I teach, there are many children of owners of small and medium companies in the student body. And, these students find that being the child of a small business owner is a disadvanatage in finding jobs. The reason, of course, is that many companies hesitate to accept these people who may leave sooner or later to take on the family business.

There was even a case of a particular student who filed for a position in a company without disclosing that his father owned a business. However, this "secret" was eventually discovered and, when that happened, the company put off its commitment in the very last stage. On another occasion, I personally met a corporate officer in charge of checking the personal and family background of potential recruits and what concerned him most was the fact that a certain candidate came from a business owner's family. I pointed out that even among those workers whose father does not own a business, there will be people who leave the company when they have decided that they have had enough. By the same token, there may be sons of small scale entrepreneurs who will stay with a company as long as they can find some significance and challenge in the task they are given there and also feel comfortable in the environment. I told the officer that the atmosphere and the attitude of the company would greatly affect such decisions of whether one leaves or not. The officer was convinced that it was "up to the company" to retain the worker and thus the student in question was accepted. On the other hand, there is even a case of a student whose father, a business owner, went around systematically to his clients and suppliers and managed to make a deal with one of them to take his son in for a few years. The father warned from the very outset that his son would leave the company after those few years.

There is no shortage of similar examples of the difficulties faced by the offspring of small business owners. This quite vividly reflects the idea that the lifetime employment system not only signifies job security for the workers but also that the company looks forward to a more or less permanent relationship with its employees. What is incredible is that such a preference by the Japanese companies is still strong today when the "bloated" corporate structure and shortage of managerial posts have become serious issues and arguments abound on selective retirement systems and establishment of upper age limits for managerial posts.

It is often explained that the age-grade pay system is a wage scheme whereby the wages deferred during the earlier years of a person's career are paid back during the latter years of his working life, i.e. when he is in the middle and old age category. If this definition can be assumed correct, then those who join the company upon graduation from school, stay on for four or five years, and subsequently leave, should be welcomed by the companies. What should be doubly appreciated is that these people have no aspirations to reach managerial posts in the future. Thus, under the present circumstances, although there may be reasons to accept these people, there seems to be no reason for avoiding such people. Nevertheless, it is a fact that many companies are not very happy about taking in children of small and medium business owners. This just goes to show that in Japan the institutional structure of companies – something that defines the way companies are run – has itself been built with the "permanence of relations" as one of its basic foundations.

3.1.1 A Structure Consisting of Core and Peripheral Workers

A company is constantly exposed to various environmental changes such as market and seasonal fluctuations of the economy in which it exists. Aside from a few lucky companies that have always been on the growth curve, most companies go through cycles of dull and busy periods brought about by any number of environmental factors surrounding the company. The company, therefore, has to see to it that its structure and mechanism maintain flexibility in responding to such circumstances. Broadly speaking, there are three ways to achieve this flexibility.

First, the company can, in response to the changes, get rid of excess labour or hire the necessary extra manpower when the need arises. The second conceivable method is for the company to retain a rather small regular staff and for this staff to generate more output through overtime or other means when there is more work and to reduce output during dull periods. The third means is to maintain a double-structure within the system consisting of the "core" staff which works on the principle of permanent relations, and the "peripheral" workforce which serves as a shock-absorber.

Traditionally, Japanese companies have mainly drawn upon the second and the third methods. Unlike the American corporate structure where the organization itself is like an aggregate of clearly-defined, individual jobs, in a Japanese company, there is considerable leeway in the job that each member is assigned to, which permits the scope to expand or shrink in accordance with the circumstances. This makes it extremely easy to control the labour output in line with increase and decrease in work. And, as was reflected in the chronic overtime phenomenon seen commonly during the high economic growth period, second method was very often used by companies in Japan.

At the same time, an organizational structure made up of a core and periphery is common among the Japanese companies. Already, earlier in history, Japanese merchants ran their shops with this double-structure form consisting of a core, i.e. those trained under the apprenticeship system and eventually becoming managerial candidates, and the periphery, i.e. middle-aged workers and casual workers hired by the branch outlets. Eventually, the practice of lifetime employment expanded to include the general employees at major companies and skilled workers who were the successors of traditional craftsmen. Furthermore, due to reasons such as the labour shortage, the need to acquire stable and high quality labour force in keeping with the mechanization progress, and the need to bring up a work force showing loyalty to the company as a means of coping with the development of labour movements, the scope expanded yet further, this time to include a portion of the factory workers. Towards the end of the Taisho Era and into the first few years of the Showa Era (i.e. roughly during the mid-1920s, or after World War I), the so-called "paternalistic management system" struck roots in Japan. It is estimated that in those days, the share of core workers to whom this lifetime employment system applied was somewhere in the realm of 20% to 30% of the entire work force of major companies in the heavy and chemical industries.

Although slight fluctuations can be seen in the proportion of this core from time to time, over the years, it has not ceased growing gradually. In particular, after the Second World War, when it became increasingly difficult to dismiss workers due to anti-dismissal struggles and stronger unions, it reached its peak. It is a well known fact that in response to this new situation, the company wasted no time in hiring single female workers to provide the periphery for the core which had grown very big. Theoretically, the female workers were also included in the framework of lifetime employment scheme. But, in practice, most of the women left the company at a relatively early stage for marriage, childbirth, etc., thus serving as the periphery to the core.

This double structure, in a slightly altered version, also exists in the operation of private universities as well. As is widely known, the faculty of a private university consists of the full-time teachers included in the lifetime employment and age-grade pay schemes and the part-time lecturers who usually hold another job somewhere else (most of them having a full-time post in other universities). These part-time lecturers, hired on an hourly basis, are different from the peripheral work force in companies in that most of them hold a full-time post elsewhere. Perhaps because of this, the hourly wages of the peripheral lecturers can remain extremely low compared to that of full-time faculty. The figure varies from one school to another, but it is commonly estimated at around one-eighth or even one-tenth of the latter. It is obvious that if the private universities could not count on these part-time lecturers, they would either have to cut drastically down on the number of classes, or radically increase the number of subjects and/or students to be handled per teacher, or hike the tutoring fee considerably, or lower the wages of its faculty and staff members sharply.

This double structure seen in the Japanese management system is subject to criticisms such as: "It is supported by the sacrifice and miserable life of part-time workers", or "It brings about social inequality". However, as can be recognized in the anti-dismissal struggle by the unions, you have no choice but to accept the existence of the peripheral work force if you want job security for the members of the organization (or, more precisely, the *core* members of the organization). Unless the freedom of laying off workers is widely accepted as with the American and European enterprises, the companies will find no other way but to form a periphery to guarantee their own survival. Depending on how one looks at it, the American and European organizations can be regarded as institutions where only those in top management comprise the core and all others make up the periphery.

Without intending to go into a moral argument, I would like to point out that if Japanese companies want to maintain the lifetime employment system in the future and also use such permanent relations with their members as a prerequisite for obtaining group-oriented mentalities and flexibility, the creation of a periphery, in one form or other, cannot be avoided. And, under such circumstances, the main question would be how to prevent social inequity, that is, to think of ways to eliminate, as much as possible, the treatment gap between the core and the periphery, and to design the periphery in such a way that the social impact on it would be minimal when it is forced to absorb impacts. We may be able to say that what brought about today's "bloated" situation was the fact that during the high growth period the core expanded rapidly and the periphery was ignored. If the result of that is unemployment of the breadwinner of a family, the social impact has turned out to be even greater.

3.1.2 Basic Framework of the Core: Long-term Secured Employment

When discussing lifetime employment as one of the features of Japanese-style management, one often encounters the following criticisms: "Not only during the days before the Second World War, but also after the war, there have been many major companies in Japan that carried out personnel reduction and dismissals due to the business situation. The lifetime employment system is not a strict tradition in Japan." Or, "Before the war, the system was applied to only a very small portion of the workers. Moving further back into history, we have had times when there was a lot of labour mobility. It is only after the war that the lifetime employment system became established in Japan." Or even, "The lifetime employment system was only an extraordinary phenomenon characterizing the high economic growth period."

It is not very productive to argue over the lifetime employment system when each one has a different image of the system in his mind. Nevertheless, when we put together the fact that Japanese-style management has a dual structure consisting of the core and periphery, that at the root of this structure is the basic framework built on the permanence of relations, that the core has been expanding over the years, and that these factors brought about various characteristic features in the Japanese management system, we must recognize the lifetime employment system as being one of the essential elements creating the unique features of Japanese-style management.

Arguments introduced at the beginning of this section are indeed statements that ignore these structural features of Japanese-style management. In order to prevent unnecessary confusion arising out of image differences coming from the connotation of the phrase, it may be worthwhile suggesting that the term "lifetime employment" be abandoned and replaced with "long-term secured employment".

3.1.3 Rotation and Supervisorism

The lifetime employment system applied to the core staff in Japanese companies is very closely connected with the characteristic features of various management formulas in Japan.

First of all, once the lifetime employment system is established, each company strives to take good care of and hold on to its employees. As a result, they have no choice but to resort to the annual batch recruitment system, keeping apace with the graduation season of schools, to acquire people for the core. This annual recruitment method not only influences the hiring practices of the companies, but it also affects the schools providing the human material, i.e. the graduates. With this system, since a company is not recruiting personnel that it needs that very moment, but rather hiring personnel on the basis of a long-term personnel plan that determines the estimated needs and age structure for the forth-coming season,* it cannot choose its potential workers on the basis of what type of skill is needed to fill certain specific posts. Therefore, the candidates are chosen as an "abstract work force" based on their personality and general knowledge and skills (which is usually thought to be reflected in their academic marks).

In this way, the recruitment customs in Japan are characterized to a great extent by the permanence of relations. Without fully considering his or her compatibility to a job, the newly recruited employee is assigned to a post upon joining the company. Unlike the American-style companies where the institutional structure is quite logically arranged on the basis of clearly defined individual tasks, work is allocated to sections and division in Japanese companies. The recruitment and personnel allocation practices mentioned above are very compatible with this nature of Japanese organizations.

By the time the new employees get more or less used to their jobs and begin to understand what is going on in the company, a new class of freshmen joins, again through the annual recruitment procedures. The former members give the lowly jobs to the newcomers and move onto jobs that are a step higher. In this way, relocations and even promotions to some extent take the form of regular personnel reshuffles and this fits in very nicely with the Japanese scheme of small-step, continual, and regular promotions. It is on the basis of this system that rotation is conducted frequently and "supervisorism" in which those with a certain amount of accumulated experience become supervisors and managers is created. This system of training managers from among the in-house staff can be looked upon as an extremely compatible practice in the Japanese-style management system where permanence of relations is an important factor.

With a view to studying the compatibility of the system of "super-visorism" let us suppose that the specialists' post system were introduced to Japanese companies on a large scale. The changes in the various environmental factors dictate the need for new specialists' posts as well

---

* In Japan, although the graduates leave school every March and start their work career in April, the students are already tested, interviewed, and committed for recruitment roughly four to six months before graduation time.

as the lack of need for some existing posts. In a case where a person with a skill that is no longer necessary to the company can still go out and sell his knowledge and talents to another company, as in the United States, the specialits' post system can probably function smoothly.

However, when it is difficult, if not impossible, to relocate to another company, as in the case of Japan with its lifetime employment system, the specialist must either make tremendous efforts to master some other usable skill or be satisfied with a lower ranking post in the company. If such circumstacnes (for which the blame cannot be pinned on any given worker) crop up often, Japanese organizations could easily find themselves in a chaotic situation. The introduction of the specialists' post system is being studied eagerly nowadays in the light of the shortage of managerial posts and an increasingly self-centred mentality among the younger generation. However, it must be remembered that the specialists' post system has features that are hard to combine with Japanese type organizations since under the Japanese-style management system rotation is eventually necessary because of the permanence of relations within the organizations. Although it may not be totally impossible to adopt the specialists' post system it may well end up being a relief measure for those who cannot reach managerial posts in the hierarchy.

Another possibility for the specialists' post system is for the system to successfully strike roots in the Japanese business world and function as a bridge between the core and the periphery or as a new type of periphery. Just as university professors, even though committed to lifetime employment to a certain extent, move from one university to another selling their expertise, if the specialists in business or industry could also polish up their knowledge and skills aiming at better positions and move from one company to another looking for posts most suitable to their talents, it would contribute to solving problems of a shortage of managerial posts in companies. It is also possible that this will develop into a system that is more compatible with the mentalities of those in the younger generation who seek to express themselves through work. However, in reality, posts that require such high-level professionalism are relatively limited and there is very little chance that these specialists will become a major force.

As long as the Japanese management system strives to keep the core which offers a group-oriented mentality and flexibility, the long-term stable employment system is likely to be maintained as its basic framework. And, with permanent relations as its root, Japanese-style management – for its core at any rate – will maintain its uniqueness, including the rotation system.

3.1.4 Permanence of Relations and Harmonious Relations

For human relations, especially when the relations are hoped to be permanent, it is desirable to have a spontaneously mutual and harmonious relationship. This was already reflected in the human relations of Japanese villages. Human relations in a traditional village are based on extremely long-term relationships. Shiro Morita has introduced a case study where he found that in a certain hamlet consisting of 47 houses, only two families were replaced by new families during the hundred years since 1877 and the total size of the hamlet still remained at 47 households after a century. (Shiro Morita, *Mura no Seikatsu-shi* (Life History in a Village), pp. 5-6) Similar observations are reported by other studies too. (e.g. Minoru Kida, *Nippon Buraku* (Japanese Hamlet), p. 183)

For many villagers in Japan, the village was for them a kind of "microcosm" and it was inconceivable for them to live outside of it. And, for generations, the villagers maintained unbelievably long-term mutual relations. In this sense, the Japanese villages differed considerably from the community villages in the Western societies, especially from those in the United States. I believe that it is in such a situation from which one could not extricate oneself that Japanese traits such as situational adaptability, stressing "familiarity" in human relations, and groupism developed.

In an unescapable long-term relationship like this, sustaining harmonious relations become very important and, for that, a comformist mentality able to suppress one's self-assertion becomes necessary. In his great work, Minoru Kida describes this point very skillfully. I would like to introduce a relatively long quote from it. This will describe very interestingly the various situations in a hamlet that are remarkably similar to situations in today's Japanese management system, such as the need for harmonious relations within an unavoidable permanent relationship, conformity that makes such harmony possible, the necessity of root-binding (*nemawashi*), and so on.

" ... Sure, majority vote may be more progressive, but it is not fit for our hamlet council. Majority vote is a decisive battle. Things we decide on here are mostly things that directly affect us. So if you lose out on a vote, that means that you have lost your argument, you are going to lose money, and if your buddies were on the other side, that's hard on you, you know? And you are never going to forget that hard feeling, no sir! And that is going to bring unpleasantness to the whole hamlet so the council really do not want to take that sort of step. It has been the tradition − for a long time now − in the hamlet council, and even in the village council, that if seven people out of ten agree, the remaining three give up their argument and also agree. This is all for good relations in the hamlet. If you just cannot make the minority say yes, then you do not vote. You continue persuading them until you have convinced them. So you always get a unanimous decision. After all, we are so small in number. If there is any division within the hamlet, not only the minority but the majority will also have less houses to visit for a cup of tea. .... " (Kida, op. cit., p. 82)

Kida also points out in the same book that this urge for unanimity is not exactly a feudalistic and deliberate means designed to suppress the minority but a reflection of the hamlet's life style, and that once there is a "crack" in the hamlet, it takes at least six months to return to the original state of harmony. (op. cit., p. 76) These points indicate how important it is to maintain harmony in a permanent relationship, and how necessary that is for "life" within any group.

These things basically fit contemporary Japanese-style management as well. Under a long-term fixed relationship, the maintenance of harmonious relations is necessary both from the viewpoint of effectively accomplishing the corporate objectives and of preserving "comfort and pleasantness" within the company. Thus, many techniques and schemes for keeping up harmonious relations are built into the Japanese management system. Various parties and trips held by each department and section, preparation of "company funds" for such events, unique decision-making process such as the *ringi* system and various forms of meetings, communication relying heavily on personal interplay rather than by written means, exclusion of elements that rock the boat and disturb harmony, all of these are part of this effort. Respect for an orderly status system and the age-grade pay scheme for avoiding sudden, dramatic changes in the ranking order are also closely connected with this. We must bear in mind that too loose an attitude in introducing the merit system may involve a danger of destroying, from the very foundation, the harmonious relationship existing under the concept of permanence of relations.

3.1.5 Maintaining Relations

The practice of respecting permanent and harmonious relations exists not only within companies in Japan but also in inter-company relations as well as company-consumer and company-client relations. There is a common Japanese phrase that goes "chance customers are not welcomed". As this statement so typically illustrates, there is a tendency among Japanese companies to avoid doing business with whom they are not "familiar". In a megalopolis like Tokyo, this tendency has give way to a great extent due to urbanization and the weakening of human r themselves. However, the tendency seems to remain very strong in small local towns and rural areas but also in big cities like O

Nagoya. Under such circumstances, developing one's business virtually means building up one's useful "familiarity" relations.

The example introduced earlier to illustrate the creation of a "familiar" relationship was in connection with sales activities. There are other examples that indicate, in a very interesting way, the degree to which the establishment of such relations affect the psychology of the Japanese people. This is a story that I heard when I was invited by a dentists' group in Tokyo to talk on "Japanese-style human relations and management system". The following comment and story comes from Dr. Shunzo Kobayashi, the organizer of the group.

According to Dr. Kobayashi, the concept of "familiarity" exists in the relationship between a dentist and his patient. Interestingly enough, those patients who are familiar with the doctor's treatment seldom complain about pain but those who come in for a treatment once in a blue moon usually express great pain. Since three friends of mine all vouch for quality of Dr. Kobayashi's dental treatment, this story goes to show that the presence (or non-presence) of "familiarity" or of "familiar trust" even affects the physical sensations of patients.

From this story, it would not be surprising if "familiar" products actually looked better in the eyes of the consumers. The fact that advertising activities by companies have gone beyond the scope of notifying the quality of the products and resort to "hard sell" tactics shows that the companies are trying to create a one-way familiarity relationship with the consumers.

Such "familiarity" relations are not something that arise exclusively in the field of marketing between a company and consumers. Japanese companies make tremendous efforts, day in and day out, to create and maintain permanent and harmonious relations based on "familiarity" with their banks, with their clients, and so on. It is probably this type of relations that Kohei Hisaeda is referring to when he speaks about "tacit agreement" and "insurance mechanism". As he points out, in North American societies, a company engages in business equipping itself with investigation results obtained through a research company and insurance in case things do not work out. On the other hand, a Japanese sits down with the people from the other party, sips tea with them, and spends a tremendous amount of time furthering communication until both parties can deal with each other openly. "This human relationship based on mutual trust forms an essential part of the Japanese-style insurance mechanism and the trust supporting such human relations is entirely personality-oriented." (Kohei Hisaeda, *Keiyaku no Shakai, Mokuyaku no Shakai*)

In the context of such "familiarity" relations in the business world, the mutual trust relations must be maintained by all means because it is not uncommon for the trust to be damaged greatly by the slightest mishap. The following is an incident that actually happened between a certain well-known company and the university where I teach.

A student who had received a provisional commitment from a first rate company to hire him betrayed the trust of that company by joining a different company. When you graduate thousands of students every year, once in a while you come across students who behave like this. Since the school did not have any authority to tie down that student to his original commitment, it could not do anything about it. But the company never forgot this incident. So, for over ten years and until very recently, the company refused to place any "new employees wanted" notices with the school despite repeated requests from the school to do so. Only very recently, did this company say that it was going to "forget about the incident" and resume recruitment from the school. This example shows how a thoughtless act by one member of an organization can impair the "familiarity" and trust relations existing between two institutions.

In order to keep up the "familiarity" relations, one often has to exert extra care and considerations so as not to hurt the other party. Much ingenuity must be displayed in adjusting mutual interests and turning down offers. The story of a capable salesman, introduced by Takao Iwasawa who is a Chief Research Worker in the Research Institute of Distribution Economy is quite interesting in this sense.

When this salesman is asked by a shopowner to take back goods that he delivered previously because they do not sell, he never resists. "Fine," he says and take the merchandise, goes around the block, and leaves them at the back door of the same shop saying, with a bow, "please look after them well." The salesman says that this method brings surprisingly better results than saying "no" to the shopowner or giving him a list of explanations as to why he cannot take them back. The idea is that you cannot be a good salesman unless you have a quick wit like this. Of course, this must have been a countermeasure that was designed on the basis of the salesman's sensitivity in reading the character and personality of the other party. This is a very revealing example of maintaining the "familiarity" relaions in business whereby one avoids an agrument with the other party, pulls back, but accomplishes the initial objective anyway.

3.2 STATUS AWARENESS
3.2.1 Egalitarian Mentality

When working for a Japanese organization, one sometimes notices a peculiar thing about the egalitarian mentality of the Japanese people. In an American university, there are great differences in salaries among the professors. Around 1970, when I was in the United States, I would often hear about professors who were scouted for an annual contract of $30,000 when it was not uncommon to find full-time professors working for an annual income of less than $20,000. It is not as if I conducted a survey on this matter so I cannot offer any exact data. Nevertheless, it is a fact that the differences were considerable.

On the other hand, in Japan, the salary of a professor who shows great enthusiasm in teaching the students and comes out frequently with excellent studies does not differ from that of a professor who has not turned out a paper in ten years. And very few people seem to consider this situation as being unfair. In fact, if the school tried to introduce even the slightest wage differentials into this situation, there would most likely be a great fuss about it. Some years ago, the question of whether head teachers in schools should be paid extra allowances became a major issue in educational circles in Japan. Although there are many factors related to this, we cannot deny the fact that the idea of an extra wage benefit conflicted with the egalitarian mentality of the Japanese and turned the opposition campaign into a very emotional one.

What is interesting here is that while the Japanese people are extremely sensitive about equality regarding wages, they are very indifferent about equality in work burden. Another point is that this egalitarian awareness concerning wages applies only to the full-fledged members of the group, i.e. the core of the organizations, and not the peripheral members. Some examples follow.

I regret to have to take an example again from the academia. In many universities, there is considerable inequality with regard to the duties of each member. Although the situation may vary from one school to another, in most cases the extra allowance paid for holding a titular post is nominal and does not really compensate for the time and effort spent on fulfilling the task, not to mention the loss from interrupting your own research work. The amount is only a drop in the bucket. Thus, these posts usually rotate from one member to the other. But the sharing of the burden is often not very fair. The competent ones usually end up being bogged down with much work and, if you can cleverly convince your colleagues of your incompetence, you may get away without being assigned to a post. What is even more interesting is that those who are not popular within the core, i.e. those who are not liked by their colleauge professors, can evade assuming the responsibility while if you are unfortunately liked by them you end up getting the post and the burden that comes with it.

The same can be said for lecturers as well. Regardless of whether you are in charge of a class in the required general course handling 500 or even 1,000 students or whether you hold a small specialized class with only a few students, both are counted as "one class". Perhaps because of the pride one feels in being in charge of an "important" class, there is even a tendency for some lecturers to hold onto "important" classes (i.e. with more students to look after, implying a heavier burden).

During meetings of university staff members, it is often suggested that they should demand wages of the same level as that of lecturers. Since the market mechanism is not in full operation in this field, it is quite difficult to define "appropriate" wages for the staff. But at any rate, while a school would suffer from a shortage of good teachers if the wages and work conditions were poor since there is some mobility of teaching personnel from one school to another, the demands of the general staff members are a bit hard to accept when, partly due to the recession, dozens of people apply for every job opening there is in this field. Moreover, when demanding an extra allowance for special work such as entrance examination work, the union files for the increased allowance on the basis of the idea that they have more work to do since there are more people taking the tests. But when it comes to the distribution of the allowance, it changes its logic and starts saying that it should be shared as equally as possible since it is a type of "living allowance". This again illustrates a characteristic feature of the egalitarian mentality of the Japanese.

Generally speaking, egalitarianism in Japanese organizations works very meticulously for distribution of the fruits of labour, but does not play an active role in the distribution of the labour itself.

Recently, while I was re-reading Hayao Shimizu's book *Nihon-jin wa Kawatta-ka* (Have the Japanese Changed?), I came across a very interesting section. In developing his elaborate analysis of egalitarianism, Shimizu explains about an intriguing concept called "physiological egalitarianism". "This boils down to the idea that since all men are equal physiologically, they shall be equal before the law, too." As an example illustrating such physiological egalitarianism, Shimizu draws upon a statement that goes, "There is indeed a capability gap between a skilled worker and an unskilled worker. But both possess the same physiological needs *as human beings.* Up until now, wages have been paid in accordance with the capability difference between the two. But from now on, the same wage should be paid for both in consideration of same physiological needs that the two have." Shimizu points out that this is not a story put together to make the readers laugh and mentions that there was an anti-establishment controversialist who actually demanded this. More specifically, Shimizu goes on to introduce the contents of the essay by Makoto Oda printed in the August 1970 issue of the magazine *Tenbo.*

Shimizu displays his sarcasm in referring to Oda as "someone who seems to dearly enjoy making jokes". This mentality seems to exist not only with Oda but widely throughout the Japanese people in differing degrees. As Shimizu points out, in most cases, people recognize the objective fact that there are differences in individual capabilities and do not feel too uncomfortable about the corporate president's high salary. Still, it does seem to be true that "physiological egalitarianism" often comes to the fore when discussing the degree of differences and how they should be expressed thus affecting the decisions on wages and conditions in Japanese organizations in no small degree. As a matter of fact, it cannot be denied that the age-grade pay system is extremely compatible with such a mentality of the Japanese people.

It is still not clear as to exactly how this egalitarianism came to strike roots in Japanese organizations. It seems quite worthwhile to briefly study the relationship between egalitarianism and factors such as *ie* (traditional Japanese family system) and *mura* (village communities).

As the relations between the head family, the branch families, and employees indicate, the *ie* system in Japan formed a type of ranking order. To the contrary, among the villagers, as Minoru Kida points out very interestingly, a unique form of egalitarianism governed their daily lives. Kida explains:

"I was impressed by the fairness and justice that the hamlet people possessed. Of course, this sort of thing could come about easily if all of the residents in the hamlet were born with fair and just minds. But that does not correspond to the observations I have made of the people whom I have studied day in and day out. Rather, in view of the realities of hamlet life, it is more realistic to say that since enthusiasm for survival and life is so strong among the hamlet people and they want to egoistically look after their own self-interest whenever there is chance and whenever it is possible to escape the notice of others, they always check on each other, and this practice of mutual supervision of what each one takes has forced people to be fair and just. The awareness of fairness and justice in this sense constantly governs every aspect of hamlet life." (Kida, op. cit., p. 70)

It is very enlightening to know that in a village, as Kida points out, "The two-dimensional mentality of 'this fellow and that fellow and myself are all equal in hamlet life' has developed to such an extent that it has formed a sensitive feeling of equilibrium, egalitarianism, and justice in the minds of the hamlet people who detest being taken advantage of by others or seeing other people gain more." (ibid.)

3.2.2 Establishment of the Age-grade Pay System

The question of how the seniority concept came into being what type of psychological foundations and under what environmental factors it appeared and how it struck roots, is an issue that still remains to be studied. Presumably, during the earlier years of Japanese-style management when the concept of *ie* was predominant, it may have been a form of expressing recognition for loyalty and contribution based on the duration of having faithfully endured severe working conditions. At the same time, in an age when status ranking was very strict, it must have been difficult to maintain internal order if the superior-inferior ranking were allowed to change suddenly. But, it is also a fact that when the authoritative power of *ie* was extremely strong, it was easy for a certain individual to be treated exceptionally well and to come out on the top. To the contrary, in the post-war society when the *ie* system was abolished and the authority accompanying it was destroyed, helped partially by a bigger say of the unions, the needs and value concepts of the employees came to be reflected greatly in the management system.

Since the age-grade pay system is a scheme directly affecting the treatment and status of the workers, this last point was especially true. For example, the so-called "living wage structure" for the post-war electric industry is the best example that clearly and typically reflects "physiological egalitarianism". The egalitarian awareness of the Japanese people started appearing clearly in the age-grade pay system developed after the Second World War. Needless to say, as the Japanese economy recovered, management gradually regained its confidence and as it restored its managerial powers it started introducing slight differentials in the living wage structure. This post-war age-grade pay system that is basically structured around the idea of seniority but with which there is a gradual incorporation of wage differentials based on other factors has made the Japanese-style age-grade pay system quite unique in that it serves as an effective and economical incentive system, bringing effective dynamism into organizations managed Japanese style. Detailed explanation on this point follows.

(i) Status Awareness of the Japanese

To study this subject, we must first look at the people's unique awareness of status in Japan as well as their concept regarding man's capabilities. With Americans and Europeans, there is a tendency to position oneself in society as an "individual" and to try to restrict mutual relations both functionally and time-wise. To the contrary, a Japanese seeks to position himself in society by "affiliating" with a group. This is clearly reflected in the way names are expressed and how addresses are written. In Western societies, one first describes the individual and then various explanations on him follow, such as saying one's given name first and then the family name. This was an effective system as long as you were living in a small community and everyone knew everyone else. But as modern society became more and more complex and institutionalized, and each individual became nothing but a tiny cog, the practice started revealing many drawbacks. This is partially reflected in the fact that for many official documents involving literally millions of names to be dealt with, people's names are expressed in the order of surname-given names even in Western societies.

The fact that importance is attached to "affiliation" in Japan is also reflected in the way names are expressed. With the *samurai* warriors among whom affiliation with the *ie* was an extremely important matter, the surname (i.e. the *ie* name) was stated first followed by their personal names. Merchants, who were prohibited from possessing surnames and carrying swords, used their store or company names like surnames and always mentioned that before their personal names, such as *"Kashima-ya Denbei"* (meaning "Denbei Kashima-Store"). In case of an employee, he would be referred to as *"Kashima-ya no Jinkichi-don"* or "Kashima-Store's lad Jinkichi". In the case of peasants, the village or hamlet name was used as their affiliation identity such as *"Yamada-mura no Tagosaku"* meaning "Yamada Village's Tagosaku (personal name)". What is interesting is that even today, the same practice is observed by people in Japan who indicate their professional affiliation before their names, such as *"Musashi Daigaku no Iwata"* ("Musashi University's Iwata"), *"Toshiba no Matsuoka"* ("Toshiba's Matsuoka"). Of course, depending on to whom you are talking, there may be cases when you indicate the name of the city or town you come from, again before your name.

As has already been explained in Chapter 2, since a Japanese person seeks to position himself in the society by means of affiliating with a given group, his main concern tends to be directed internally towards the group and his interest in the broader society becomes indirect and weak. This creates a very unique characteristic in the Japanese people's awareness of status. Externally, since the Japanese people position and evaluate each other on the basis of the group they are affiliated with, they tend to become extremely sensitive about the social prestige of the group. At the same time, they become particularly sensitive about status relations within the group they are affiliated with. So, it is correct to say that the Japanese people's awareness of status tends to consist of two things; an awareness of the status of the group, and an awareness of the individual status relations within the group. This tendency has been accelerated as the affiliation awareness of the Japanese moved from a simple structured community-oriented one to an occupational-oriented one consisting of a complex class structure and mutually differing prestige.

At the same time, the egalitarian awareness of the Japanese people which we studied in the foregoing pages is reflected not only in wage-related matters but also in the status concept of the people. Among the

Japanese, there is a tendency to thoroughly loathe the idea of introducing even the slightest differentials in the treatemnt of personnel within an organization. Generally speaking, for a company to effectively attain its business objectives, you need some sort of a command and order mechanism and this naturally implies a type of class structure. This is clear from the fact that even in American and European societies where equal civil rights is the basic prerequisite of society (in theory, at any rate), companies cannot do without a strict class structure. Since the Japanese people possess a unique egalitarian concept, there is a tendency to strongly resist or react to status differences within the organization. And such a mentality of the members ends up being reflected in the corporate management approach. The age-grade pay system can be regarded as one of the methods that generated the least resistance from the egalitarian minds of the Japanese people. That is because the system, while creating those who command and those who are ordered about, can be interpreted as merely a ladder of rankings that everyone will eventually climb, not a rigid status system. At the same time, because of the "physiological egalitarianism" of the Japanese people, there is little resistance to living wages received this way. The age-grade pay system can be regarded as a scheme well suited to the egalitarian concept of the Japanese people.

Since management introduced the system of slowly incorporating slight differentials into the age-grade pay system that is based on a continual promotion scheme, and because of the Japanese mentality of being extremely sensitive about status relations within the organization, these slight differentials became a very strong stimulus in Japanese organizations bringing a keen competition and dynamism into Japanese organizations.

(ii) Japanese Concept of Man's Capabilities

The concept of man's capabilities as conceived by the Japanese, as well as the uniqueness of Japanese-style competition created by that concept, also seems to stimulate the intra-organizational race for promotions. Words and phrases like "capability" and "merit system based on ability" tend to be used too often without taking into consideration their full meaning. Here, I wish to point out the necessity of distinguishing between two different concepts that the word "capability" connotes. The two are: (1) the level of capability reached through training and/or experience; and (2) the capability that one possesses as potential power. I will refer to the former as "ability" and the latter as "capability" and also use the word capability (without quotation marks) when referring to the broad concept covering both connotations. (Basically, the system of determining one's pay and treatment on the basis of "ability" is called the merit system. I feel that the Japanese system of determining treatment based mainly on one's "capability" is different from the so-called merit system but a type of capability-oriented pay scheme.)

In American society, as compared to Japan, there is a general tendency to focus mainly on "ability". In this type of a society, the idea that someone is capable of doing something means that this capability can be displayed right away. At the same time, it is something that is recognized only in connection with a given scope of activities. This idea of capability is clearly reflected in American-style personnel practices, in particular the hiring practices. To the contrary, in the Japanese context, the word capability carries two unique nuances. (1) Capability is often understood as something vague and general; (2) Capability is often interpreted as "capability", i.e. potential capacity that is to be further developed by training and experience, not "ability".

Because of this reason, it is often thought in Japan that while a "capable" person is "capable" of doing anything well, the "incompetent" is not good no matter what he is given to do. Therefore, in Japan, because of its general nature, capability tends to dominate an important position in evaluating a person and the existence or non-existence of capability directly affects the human value of that person. Also, because of its "potentiality" concept, success is often regarded as a proof of that person's immeasurable "capability". This injects unique features into competition in Japanese society.

First of all, the Japanese tend to get deeply involved in competition. Losing out in a competition is considered a proof of one's incompetence or proof of being an inferior human being. It is even a defeat in one's life. Secondly, proving one's "capability" is a very important aspect in competition. And when the difference in "capabilities" become obvious, the competition is considered to be over at that stage. Thirdly, once a person is recognized as having proven his "capability", that person finds himself in an extremely advantageous position vis-a-vis his opponent. He no longer has to prove his "capability" repeatedly. The only thing required of him is to polish up his "capability".

I feel that the college entrance examination race that Japan has become so famous typically illustrates such features of Japanese-style competition. The Japanese practice of placing too great stress on one's educational background is also probably endorsed by this concept of capability. And since it is so deep-rooted, it cannot be readily eliminated. Further analysis of this issue will be saved for another occasion.

The foregoing brief explanation is probably enough to show that the Japanese awareness of status, egalitarianism, and the unique concept of capability as well as the idea of competition arising out of it, result in keen competition under the present age-grade pay system where differentials are delicately incorporated bit by bit. The age-grade pay system is a form of capability-oriented system (or "merit system" in the broad sense) that fits in with Japanese society. What is important here is that, in this type of a race, people compete with one another with each of them having the possibility to rise, that, since the wage differentials are incorporated into the system very slowly, more members are kept in the race for longer peiods of time thus bringing about greater dynamism, and that by introducing the minimum differentials, the shock is dampened, making this an effective yet economically cheap incentive system taking full advantage of the Japanese people's urge for status. If the companies had introduced a system under which gaps appeared rapidly, because of the Japanese concept that competition is over once the "capability" difference becomes obvious, many people would withdraw from the race at an early stage, taking with them strong feelings of frustration and discouragement which in turn would have hindered their group-oriented mentality.

In an organization where long-term relations are expected on the basis of the lifetime employment system, the accumulation of the slightest differentials will eventually become decisive and thus it is enough to serve as an incentive. On the other hand, sudden changes in the ranking order involve a danger of destroying harmonious relations, namely the kind of relations that are needed for a permanent relationship. We often hear about a female employee who wept in frustration because her monthly salary was lower than her colleague's by a couple of hundreds of yen (a dollar or so). In the case of male workers, who devote the most important working years of their lives to the company, the frustration at being evaluated lowly in the organization must be more than words can express, although they may not reveal this to anyone.

The age-grade pay system which has often been the target of criticism by many economists and business critics has, for all practical purposes, been serving as a unique incentive system that conforms with the Japanese mentality and has effectively displayed its effect. Of course, the degree of the effect varies from one company to another, and since many other factors are involved, I do not mean to advocate that the system has worked efficiently in all types of organizations. Nevertheless, when we look at the age-grade pay system as one kind of pattern that successfully struck roots deeply in Japanese-style management, it can be recognized as a cleverly designed system that is well adapted to the Japanese management climate.

3.3 DIFFERENCES BETWEEN AMERICAN-EUROPEAN AND JAPANESE ORGANIZATIONS

3.3.1 Machine Model: American and European Type Organizations are Based on Rationality of Strategies and Systems

In a society where the organization members would not know what to do unless they are given concrete job specifications, an organization is structured in such a way that clearly defined tasks, each of which can be accomplished by an individual, are built on top of each other so that the aggregate of these tasks would end up uniting to attain the organizational objectives.

The famous Normandy landing, implemented under the command of General Eisenhower, is a good example of such a concept being upgraded to the highest level and applied even to military tactics. This, of course, is an example of a glorious success. But let us assume that the reverse occurred. Let us suppose that boxes where drawn onto a soccer field, the number of such boxes being equal to the number of players on the field, and also assume that each player was not allowed to step out of his box. This must result in a very different type of a soccer game. If both teams abided by this same rule, a new type of soccer game may be created. However, if one team played the conventional way, i.e. the players moving about freely, it would be interesting to see what sort of a game would result.

At any rate, with American and European type organizations, a thoroughly precise structure is necessary in order to implement the business strategies devised by top management. And it can be assumed that a large portion of the burden and responsibility for structuring and mobilizing the organization rests with top management. That is to say, the top management of a big American or European organization is like a giant putting all its efforts into moving an enormous, non-automatic, precision machine, that does not always move smoothly. This machine has, to date, been running pretty well, despite little squeaks here and there.

Such an organization is made up of various parts and components and the members comprising it are considered to be, so to speak, replaceable parts. If a vacancy arises, it is immediately filled. If a gear is not operating smoothly, it is immediately replaced with a new one. The transmission of the driving force from the motor, i.e. top management, to the end units is accomplished by the function of authority. From the viewpoint of "organic function" of institutions, they are pretty awkward and stiff as organizations go. Of course, not all of American and European organizations fit this description one hundred percent. But it is a fact that the effort to make organizations take this bureaucratic structure is something that the American and European managers or entrepreneurs have systematically sought until very recently. It was also the basic picture of American-style business and management theories. It was the science of human relations that was offered as an antithesis to this way of interpreting organizations. It is very interesting to note that even the Hawthorne Experiments, which marked the beginning of human relations science, depended upon the concept of machine model.

The other view is the management theory introduced by M.P. Follett. Follett's idea, which stresses the importance of appropriate behaviour vis-a-vis the "situations" in active departments that are constantly in contact with the corporate environment as well as the importance of intra-departmental coordination, offered a humble yet significant antithesis to the genealogy of management theories based on the machine model concept. And, it was C.I. Barnard who formulated a gigantic comprehensive model based on this new wave of thoughts. However, it remains uncertain to what extent Barnard's theory, which had such a significant impact in Japanese academic circles that the phenomenon came to be expressed as the "Barnard Revolution", actually influenced the companies in the United States. The answer will perhaps come in the future.

In practice, the concept of the machine model seems to remain the basic mainstream of ideas supporting organizational activities in Western societies, especially in North America. Since I myself am not well versed in the history of management theories, I shall avoid going deeper into this subject but rather offer observations on Japanese organizations in comparison with the American and European models.

3.3.2 Human Co-working Model: In Japanese Orgnaizations, Everyone Thinks Together and Tries Together

In contrast to such American and European-type organizations, Japanese organizations represent what one might call a human co-working model. First of all, the members of the organization are not considered replaceable parts that merely perform designated tasks. The members that make up the core of an organization are generally regarded as "colleagues" that work together, under permanent relations, until retirement age, to attain the organizational objectives. In most cases, after joining a company, one is shifted around from one section to another at short intervals. The person accumulates a variety of experience in those sections, hands down the lowly jobs each year to the new batch of freshmen joining the organization, and in this way gradually masters various jobs. Throughout the process, he forms a network of friendly relations, in various forms, with many other members of the same organization, builds up his information network, and accumulates knowledge on in-house situations and history.

In this way, he creates an attitude or action pattern that enables him to respond quickly to all sorts of situations, with slight variations from one individual to another. And, in this way, he turns himself into an "indispensable colleague", something very different from being a replaceable part. Theoretically speaking, there actually *is* considerable replaceability even under this system. However, in Japanese organizations, these "indispensable" colleagues are favoured more than the newcomers who are not too familiar with the in-house situations. Here, again, the maintenance of permanent relations is thought to be desirable.

In most cases, these "colleagues" work together under a flexibly structured job scheme. An organization is comprised of various groups, the groups being sections, departments, bureaus, etc. In other words, each section or department is held responsible for accomplishing a certain group task. The distribution of work and responsibility within each section (or whatever unit) is determined by the manager of the unit, in accordance with the prevailing circumstances. This is adjusted quite flexibly depending on the total amount of work, distribution of ability within the work force, and other factors. Even after the work is distributed and each person is notified of his share of the burden, he is expected to help out the others, even if that means putting aside his own job temporarily, should circumstances require him to do so. In other words, people are co-working under a very "loose" definition of "roles" keeping a flexible attitude towards various situations.

In a Japanese organization, the assorted group units making it up are structured in such a way that they act quickly in any given situation, just like a soccer team. Whereas an American or European organization is like a precision machine made up of a combination of parts that do not have self-mobility capabilities, a Japanese organization is like an organism that consists of cells, i.e. sections and departments, that cannot exist independently but do act on their own to some extent in accordance with the situations that come up.

If we view the American and European managers as giants trying with all their might to move a gigantic precision machine with no self-mobility, Japanese managers can be regarded as something like a nerve centre that regulates various parts of the anatomy to maintain good physical condition and health. The comment by Koji Kobayashi, Chairman of Nippon Electric Company, which has already been quoted in Chapter 2 illustrates this difference very clearly. Whereas in Japanese companies, even if the management does not spell out its orders, on the basis of tacit understanding the people working for the company try to think of ways that would be of advantage to the company, in American and European companies the management will be criticized if it does not issue clear and specific orders to the employees. The following further comments by Mr. Kobayashi highlight this point even further.

"Half of the former chairmen and presidents of American companies I know have died of heart attacks after retiring at 65. . . . In other words, the higher you are in the hierarchy, the heavier your responsibilities are. Of course, we feel the great pressure of our responsibilities, too, but since I am 71 and still alive, I cannot help but suspect that the degree of pressure is not quite the same. . . . Our pressures are, although not in any irresponsible way, dispersed. . . . " (*Nihon Keizai Kenkyu Center Bulletin,* No. 322, p. 34)

In a Japanese organization where everyone thinks together and each member of a section or department cooperates and makes efforts for his group, harmonious relations based on mutual goodwill and trust are considered the ideal and that requires that each member show cooperativeness, if not wholeheartedly, at least on the surface. This has introduced various features into the Japanese organizations that are not found in American or European systems.

Chapter 4

DYNAMISM AND EFFICIENCY OF JAPANESE ORGANIZATION

4.1 DYNAMISM

4.1.1 The Age-grade Pay System and Intra-organizational Promotion Race

The following story was told by a close friend of mine when I was still a student. There is a local newspaper read by the residents of his hometown in one of the beautiful islands on the Inland Sea. The local newspaper publisher sponsors a beauty contest every year. This by itself is not really anything special. But it is the way the contest is held that is most intriguing. This newspaper is a small local establishment and its financial situation is not exactly what you would call comfortable. So, the beauty contest is a desperate means of fund raising for it.

The readers of the paper are given the right to vote in this contest. The voting slip is printed on the newspaper. As soon as the contest seasons begins, the paper begins periodically releasing "news flashes" to report the number of votes the candidates have collected so far. Every year, the paper selects daughters of leading village figures who have lots of relatives and friends, in other words, girls from "good" families, and creates a tug-of-war through its frequent "news flashes," with one girl ahead at one time and the other girl taking the lead later on. Villagers who may not be that interested at the outset eventually get involved in the race and the excitement gradually builds up. In particular, the parents and relatives of the candidates even regard it as a point of honour to help the girl to victory. Thus, a rat race begins to purchase the newspaper and get hold of the voting slips. The same thing happens with the other girl's relatives and supporters and the newspaper all of a sudden boosts tremendous sales. While the readers get excited over the whole event, the poor girls appear in a tight contest on paper. At about the time that people have grown tired of this, the newspaper publisher crowns one of them as the queen.

Every time I take up the subject of the age-grade pay system and the merit system, this story comes to my mind. What would happen if an unsurmountable gap appeared in the very early stages of this contest? The competing groups would quickly lose their ethusiasm and the newspaper would not sell that well. It is because the race is very tight and nobody knows for sure what the outcome will be that people display their competitiveness and become absorbed in the contest.

In many Japanese companies, during the first ten years or so of one's career with the company, individual wage differentials (between those members with the same number of career years) are seldom introduced even if performance evaluations are conducted. In the years that follow, slight differentials are introduced but they are, in fact, very minimal. Moreover, since a variety of allowances and fringe benefits are added to one's salary (depending on the family structure and type of work), it is very difficult to tell who is evaluated higher unless you find a way to compare *only* the basic pay. So, when you reach a managerial post, especially the level of section manager (which, in a typical Japanese company, can take about 20 years), you finally begin to recognize slight individual differences in the number of years it took to reach the same level or in the prestige of the title that is granted. Only then do you get even a vague idea of where you are in the promotion race. Very slight differentials that would never function as an incentive in American and European organizations play a crucial role in Japanese companies.

That is because even the slightest gap eventually ends up being significant, even decisive, in Japanese companies where a permanent relationship is one of the essential factors. In addition, the unique concepts of egalitarianism, capabilities, and status awareness that make the Japanese highly sensitive about their status within the organization help these slight differentials to function even more effectively as incentives. Because of this, the Japanese system of age-grade pay, which at one time was criticized as being a disincentive for the workers, has actually been arousing very keen competition for promotion in Japanese organizations. And, because the differentials are so small, more members stay in the race for longer periods of time thus helping the organization maintain its dynamism. It also offers an economical low-cost incentive system for Japanese-style management.

4.1.2 The Group Structure and Inter-group Competition within Organizations

Taking advantage of the natural group orientation of the Japanese, organizations in Japan show a kind of group-based structure. Work is not distributed to individuals as assignments but rather allocated to each group within the organization, namely a section, a department, a bureau, and so on, hereafter referred to simply as "departments.". To conduct the task assigned to the group effectively, various measures are taken within each department to enhance the group awareness of the members and to motivate them.

As a result of these measures, Japanese organizations end up containing many groups as sections and departments are established to make up the working organizational structure of the entity. This setup often creates a number of defects such as inter-departmental conflicts and delay of decision-making processes caused by such struggles. The most prominent examples of this are the budget-grabbing struggles and the wasteful spending and ineffective projects devised just to maintain a certain level of budget spending as practised in such non-commercial organizations as the bureaucracy and universities. However, when organized intelligently, this type of structure creates inter-departmental competition for the attainment of business objectives, which is a truly unique Japanese type of dynamism, within the organizations. This has helped tremendously to prevent the petrification of organizations that is often the consequence of expanding the organization into a gigantic entity.

While the promotional race within the organization brought about by the age-grade pay system is a solitary race between the individual members of the organization, it is also a "compulsory" race under which defeat brings about unconsolable frustration, deep dissatisfaction and an inferiority complex, making it one of the very few factors that creates an "uncomfortable working atmosphere" within the Japanese management system. On the other hand, the race between the groups is of such a nature that the members can enjoy its game-like aspect, like the penant races of professional baseball teams, aiming to attain goals that are constantly renewed. This particular aspect is an extremely important point when evaluating the introduction of the Western-type "merit system" in Japanese organizations, a debate that has arisen due to the recent shortage of managerial posts. This will be taken up later in the book.

The mentality of the Japanese supporting such a type of competition is clearly evident even among children and young people. My limited experience in teaching English to children has clearly shown this. There were often cases where children who used to show a very dull reaction during English lessons would all of a sudden arrive in class with shining eyes, participate actively, raise their hands often to reply, and start complaining that they were not being called on enough. This would happen very suddenly one day, as if I had poked a beehive. What I had done was to design ways for the children to clearly see the pace of progress using, for example, the point system or drawing bar graphs. I also divided the children into a number of groups, and made the groups compete with each other. Generally speaking, Japanese children are very frightened about making mistakes (many children give their answers to a question only after checking with the teacher, "Is it all right if the answer isn't correct?") and thus tend to be shy and withdrawn.

But, as soon as the inter-group race has begun, they change so much that you wonder if you are still dealing with the same children. Some of them even find the game so exciting that they arrive in the classroom half-an-hour before the starting time. When you conduct a class by forming groups with each group consisting of some bright children and some not-so-bright ones, perhaps driven by a sense of responsibility towards the group, the not-so-bright children make efforts to learn as much as possible from their brighter schoolmates and thus the learning efficiency is greatly enhanced. The educational effect of visual representation of progress towards an attainable goal has been proven among American and European children as well. What seems to be unique with Japanese children is that, while they are not so interested in the measurement of individual progress, they respond very strongly to a group evaluation of progress.

Although they will make some efforts on the basis of an individual evaluation, this tends to be accepted as a "forced" effort since it is accompanied by the feeling of "I can't put myself in an *embarrassing* position by lagging behind the others." And, under this system, once a gap is created, the one lagging behind tends to lose enthusiasm and drop out of the race completely.

This kind of attitude among the Japanese appears already among first and second graders in primary school (6 and 7 years old). The tendency continues to show strongly in a "cheerful" manner until the children reach their fifth year of primary school. By the time they reach junior high school, a simple group race to compare the results of learning fails to arouse their enthusiasm. This is perhaps because, already at this stage, an individual race begins in preparation for the high school and college entrance examinations. Nevertheless, the tendency of the Japanese to enjoy inter-group competition does not completely disappear even well into adulthood.

At the apartment complex I live in, we often have families in the building take part in making flower beds. On such occasions, a person acting as the supervisor (usually self-appointed) goes around from bed to bed instilling enthusiasm in the people. "Come on, now! It's a race to see which block's flower bed will be the prettiest." My personal reaction to such words is "Huh! Treating us like children! What a rude fellow." But the supervisor always seems to be satisfied with the booster effect of his words and continues patrolling the beautifully decorated beds.

This mentality of the Japanese people is fully utilized in Japanese companies in various forms and contributes in no small degree to sustaining corporate dynamism.

4.1.3 Dynamism Brought About by Flexibility of Organization

When I was still a student, a noted American economist Leo Huberman visited Japan and gave a lecture at the University of Tokyo. Although I must admit I have forgotten most of the lecture, there is one part that has remained distinctly in my memory to date. It was about his trip to India and went as follows.

During his stay in India, the professor went to the post office to mail a letter. The postal employee at the counter was obviously a government official and came from a high caste. It was beneath him to do something so vulgar as to "lick" the stamps with his tongue. (Recently, such vulgar acts seem to have disappeared in Japan as well.) According to the professor, this exalted government official made his servant bring water and then happily pasted the stamps on the envelope. It was like this for everything, making the whole process very inefficient and obviously it took a long time just to mail a letter. His wife, who fortunately happened to go to the next counter, was attended by a young British woman who took care of her letter quickly. Maybe it was because I listened to this story with a bit of surprise that I remember it so well.

The fact is that even in European countries and the United States where Dr. Huberman, who was so shocked by his experience in India, comes from, there is no shortage of stories concerning inefficiency. I do not know whether the following extreme example is an actual story or only a joke reflecting the recent feelings of middle class Americans about the unions which are associated more closely to the word "monopoly" than big business in the United States. At any rate, similar examples are bound to exist all over.

A certain man commissioned a carpenter and a painter to do some repair work on his house. The painter arrived first and started his work. He soon came to a section where he had to do some very simple carpentry work because nails were sticking out and could not be coated over. So, the painter stopped his work, waited for the carpenter to arrive and, only after the carpenter got there somewhat late and hammered in the nails, did the painter resume his work. Of course, the man had to pay quite a lot of money to the painter, including payment for the time he just sat around waiting for the carpenter.

It is not clear whether this story reflects one aspect of unionism or a thought pattern of people in Western societies. Taking into account the fact that similar phenomena do occur even when a union is not involved, it may well be the latter. Tadashi Mito, in his study on the differences between Japanese management and Western management, mentions the following.

"They will not do anything aside from the specified jobs. For example, if you ask a typist who happens to be free to type out addresses on envelopes, she will not do it. And, if you order her to do it anyway, she will ask for a raise or say she is going to quit. They will not help with other people's work. No matter how busy their neighbours are and how free they may be, they will not help their neighbours. For example, between the picker who picks up parts in a warehouse and the packer who packs those parts, there is no helping one another no matter how busy the other party may be. Also, when unloading packages from a truck, no matter how urgent those packages are and no matter how unoccupied the people around the truck are, they will just stand around and look at the operation and would not extend a helping hand. . . ." (*Oyake to Watakushi*, p. 14)

To the contrary, Japanese people who are accustomed to many types of jobs because they have been rotated from place to place in the organization can fill in for someone else easily when that person happens to be absent or unavailable. In Japan, it is not uncommon to hear stories about an ex-operator plant manager stepping in to do some welding work during his patrol around the plant when he sees that a process has gotten bogged down due to an absent welder.

This kind of flexibility exists not only within the organizations but with regard to client service. The following description by Koji Kobayashi clearly spells this point out.

"For example, (in Japan) someone will deliver a piece of equipment manufactured by his company to a client and set it up for the client. In this case, an engineer would probably make the delivery himself or at least go along to explain the technicalities of the machinery. While he is at it, he would also do the soldering and wiring work for the client. This, in a way, is a free service. If he did this in the United States, he would probably be breaching the union regulations. You would have to get in touch with the wiring workers union and have them send an electrician qualified to do the work. . . ." (*Nihon Keizai Kenkyu Center Bulletin,* No.322, p. 41)

The Japanese organization in which the members accurately judge what is being demanded of them at a given time on the basis of the situation and personnel available at that moment and cooperate to effectively attain the organizational objectives is certainly endowed with the kind of dynamism that a soccer team has. Just how amazed a Westerner is at seeing such flexibility among the Japanese as described by Ryohei Magota in one of his experiences during his detention in the South Seas right after World War II.

"What astonished him was the skillfullness of the Japanese who, while engaging in road construction work, would repair automobiles and even do carpentry work when asked to by British officers. The Japanese would do jobs that were not even ordered of them. Each one of us could do some carpentry work under the rotation system. In addition, we would know how to 'cheat' cleverly where it could not be detected. We were extraordinarily good with figures, multiplying and dividing at a tremendous speed, and would make the British officer look bad when unloading freight. To the British viewpoint rooted in inflexibility, where the soldiers in charge of driving and of maintenance were completely separated and most drivers could not do any maintenance work, we must have looked slightly weird so that they sometimes complained of us as being too 'clever'. . . ." (*Nenko Chingin no Shuen* (An End to the Age-Grade Pay), Nikkei Shinsho, p. 15)

4.2 EFFICIENCY AND EFFECTIVENESS
4.2.1 Efficiency

It is very difficult to deal with the question of "efficiency" of an organization. One reason is that this issue implies a number of different perspectives for making comparisons. For example, it could be taken up from the angle of comparing the efficiency of American-style management in general – within which there must be a vast range of efficiency – against the efficiency of Japanese-style management in general. Or, it could also be taken up from the angle of comparing the efficiency when American-style management is implemented in the Japanese society against the efficiency of traditional Japanese-style management.

In the case of the former, in addition to the style of the organizations themselves, the national mentality of the people which affects the qualities of labour serves as a crucial factor. For the latter, since the framework of a company is the combination of many management methods, it does not mean that even when it has been proven that the traditional Japanese management system is efficient, the more Japanese it is, the more efficient it is. This is what makes the discussion of this subject difficult.

The second difficulty we face is that even when Japanese companies are known to function efficiently, so many factors influence it in such a complex manner that it is hard to define what percentage of the success is attributable to the organizational system or the management method itself.

Thirdly, reflecting such difficulties, conceptual tools to analytically study this issue have not been developed to any satisfactory degree, making it even more complicated to deal with this issue. Therefore, for the time being, we have to rely to some extent on judgements based on our "senses" such as to study unique case examples as we will be doing in the following pages. Here, I would like to touch upon a few points that are probably crucial in studying this matter.

In the past, I expressed my view on this issue as follows. "I personally believe that, until very recently, Japanese-style management has been functioning efficiently. The basic element of success was the creation of organizations that conform to the mentality of the Japanese and make clever use of that mentality." (*Nihon Keizai Kenkyu Center Bulletin,* No. 322, p. 36) I held this view because, as our discussions showed, high work morale is created under the Japanese-style management and it also functions promptly and flexibly according to the needs of the situation. Furthermore, the Japanese-style age-grade pay system under which slight differentials are introduced gradually turns out to be a very effective and economical low-cost incentive system.

The next example also helped support my views. While I was staying in the United States, I happened to visit a bed-ridden man. This senior citizen, upon hearing that I was from Japan, told me that his son, whom he is very proud of, was an engineer working for GE. This son recently visited Japan and found that a Japanese company under a tie-up with GE had made a plant in Japan with the same machinery and layout as the GE plant in the United States. However, the productivity in the Japanese plant turned out to be much higher. In this particular example, the technological level and other conditions must have been more or less the same for the two so the big difference in the outcome could be assumed to have come from the style of management.

Quite a similar example is also introduced by R.T. Johnson and W.G. Ouchi about a certain electronics factory in Atlanta, Georgia. Here, there is an assembly line where 35 female workers are assembling transistor panels in a predetermined process. Another assembly line of the same company, 6,000 kilometers away using the same techniques, the same number of personnel, and the same number of processes, is turning out the same parts. The only difference is the productivity between the two. The authors say that the Japanese workers at the Tokyo plant have about a 15% higher productivity than their American counterparts. The authors go on to explain that this figure is not surprising since so much has been reported on the Japanese 'productivity miracle.' Nevertheless, since this fact is being observed repeatedly in San Diego, California and all over the United States, the American managers are apparently starting to wonder if they cannot get a better idea of what the secret of this Japanese productivity is. (See *Made in America – Under Japanese Management –* translated by Masaomi Kondo and published in Japanese as *America de Seiko Suru Nihon-shiki Keiei,* *"nihon-jin no Genten,"* Shibundo, p. 89)

They also mention that at the San Diego Plant of Sony Corporation, the American workers are attaining the same productivity as at a similar plant in Japan. This leads us to assume that the factor bringing about the big productivity difference is not so much the difference between the Japanese and the American workers but between the forms of management of the two countries.

In response to such a view of mine, Masumi Tsuda, Professor at Hitotsubashi University, comments as follows.

"I have doubts about the view that Japanese-style management has been very efficient. True, the companies themselves have displayed efficiency. But you have to ask yourself which power was greater: the efforts of the corporate management itself or the various factors outside of the companies that supported the company management?" (*Nihon Keizai Kenkyu Center Bulletin,* No. 322, p. 38)

Among the external factors that helped corporate activities, Tsuda mentions protectionist measures that aroused criticism from abroad and led to capital and trade liberalization, financial policies that promoted smoother corporate operations, the fact that Japan could avail itself of cheap energy by switching from coal to oil, that high-level technologies could be easily imported, and that there were abundant sources of young and low-cost labour available. Indeed, these external factors must have played a major role and since it is difficult to separate the influence of external factors from internal factors, differences of interpreting this point cannot be avoided. Yet, when dealing with the question of management efficiency, we are not asking which of the two, i.e. the external factors or the internal factors, had a greater effect. We are taking up as an issue the efficiency of the management itself. Even if we accept the fact that the impact of the external factors was greater, we still have to deal with the question of the efficiency of the management system itself.

At this point, we do encounter one problem. Japanese companies, especially during the high growth period, clearly showed a tendency to mobilize vast amounts of manhours by various means such as having the employees put in lots of overtime or keeping them on the alert at all times, so as to add even a little bit more to the final result so that it would not end up a loser in the competition with other organizations. If we regard this great amount of labour supplied as the "input", Japanese companies cannot necessarily be regarded as having been extremely efficient. It might be considered that Japanese management took an organization that could theoretically function efficiently and used it in such a way that it lowered the efficiency simply to win out in Japanese-style competition. This happened because competition in Japan is not competition for higher investment returns but for higher ranking and/or market share in the industry. At the root of this, we can point to the existence of a unique concept of the "enterprise" which is quite different from that of Western societies, especially that of the United States.

On the other hand, Tsuda claims that the question of efficiency should be studied and compared using the same economic yardstick regardless of whether the society is oriental or occidental. At the same time, he says, "During the latter half of the 1950s and the first half of the 1960s, the real growth in the Japanese economy was always clearly above real wages. In other words, productivity was high. In that sense, we can recognize that there was efficiency."

Here, we come across a new probem. That is, from an American and European point of view, the fact that Japan has maintained high productivity on the macro level, by putting in massive manhours (by Western standards at any rate), means that labour that should naturally be compensated (at least by Western standards) exists as unpaid labour in Japan. And it is this free labour that has a lot to do with Japan's high productivity. Tsuda expresses his view as follows.

"If high efficiency is being supported by correspondingly large quantities of labour and if that labour is free; I have doubts as to what extent we can conduct an accurate discussion on whether the efficiency of Japanese management is higher or lower than that of American and European management. ..." (*Nihon Keizai Kenkyu Center Bulletin,* No. 322, p. 40)

On this, Koji Kobayashi thinks that although it is not clear to what extent the effect of such factors is shown, activities like QC and VE imply that the workers are using their brains during working hours. Although there may be a point in arguing that this means twice as much work since the workers are engaging in physical work and intellectual work at the same time, one cannot make a point of it otherwise since even if they did think about it outside of their working hours, it would be very minimal.

As far as I can see, Kobayashi's view is closer to reality with regard to blue collar workers. However, when we look at white collar workers, Tsuda's point cannot be ignored. In a white collar working environment, many companies permit the baneful custom of maintaining a situation under which work cannot be finished without putting in overtime and at the same time laying down rules to restrict overtime, thus forcing the employees to "voluntarily" waive their right to ask for appropriate overtime payment. Moreover, activities such as enhancing mutual communications, collecting information, upgrading morale, and educating employees, all of this over a drink after working hours, are being pursued all the time on a company-wide scale between the managers and subordinates or among the managers. Company parties, trips, and athletic outings can also be considered as contributing to managerial objectives in a broad sense. The time consumed for these cannot be ignored when discussing efficiency.

What is important, however, is that these activities outside of regular working hours were never imposed on people. In fact, Japanese employees often enjoy such "extra-curricula" activities and it is doubtful if one can go around calling them "unpaid labour" based on the Western way of thinking.

The concept of labour among the Japanese people is quite different from that of Americans and Europeans. For the latter, the purpose of work for each individual is totally separated from the corporate objectives and thus the main concern is to earn as much as possible by working as little as possible.

As has been repeatedly mentioned, for a Japanese, his main circle of friends and colleagues comes from the same company and his life outside the organization he belongs to is extremely limited. Thus, one's working life represents a large portion of one's whole life. So, for many Japanese, it is a joy to work together with his colleagues and an even greater joy to be highly regarded by them. In this way, the concept of work is very different from that of the Westerners. In other words, for the Japanese work and play are not completely separated from one another. Therefore, rather than a style of working only during the prescribed working hours and using the rest of the time for one's private life, most Japanese prefer working like the dickens when things are busy and then taking it easy when things are dull. Nor do they mind thinking about work outside of office or factory hours. If we accept this fact, then such a work pattern is indeed most preferable for them and it is rather unrealistic to define this as "unpaid labour" based on the Western philosophy. Moreover, if most Japanese prefer this kind of a work pattern, a management system that makes full use of such an orientation can be regarded as a system that functions efficiently in the Japanese society.

4.2.2 Effectiveness

Lastly, in connection with the question of efficiency, I would like to touch upon the question of the effectiveness of organizations in attaining organizational objectives. In addition to the question of efficiency which is measured by the ratio between input and output, we have the question of "effectiveness" towards the organizational objectives that cannot be attained by other organizations even if they wished to.

For example, Gen Itasaka describes the American workers' laziness in his book *Aa Amerika, Kizudarake no Kyozo* (America! The Scarred Virtual Image), (Kodansha Shinsho), by taking the automobile industry as an example. "In the American automobile industry, there are many workers with low working morale who do not show up on Mondays and Fridays. The vacancies are often filled by student part-timers." Because of the overall low working morale, they do not even care if they drop a couple of nuts or bolts and just let the car on the conveyor belt go by. It makes no difference to the workers that that particular missing bolt may cause a fatal accident. Consequently, people in the United States half jokingly say that you should not buy cars made on Mondays and Fridays.

Japaneses manufacturers, to the contrary, turn out goods that we can use feeling assured of their quality, and this at low cost. In other words, from the viewpoint of effectiveness in attaining management objectives as well, Japanese management has been showing a good record. Needless to say, we cannot totally ignore the external factors that led to this. But the main contributor seems to have been the style of Japanese-type management.

The aforementioned comment by Mito on the Japanese-style decision-making mechanism is very interesting from the viewpoint of the effectiveness of organizations as well. He describes the role of "system organizers" such as the *sogo shosha* (trading companies) as being "possible only under Japanese-style management where everyone above middle-management has his own communication network and functions as a decision-making centre." Mito's following additional comment seems to illustrate the effectiveness of Japanese organizations vividly.

"Therefore, no matter how competent a person is, regardless of whether he has graduated from Harvard, Oxford, or Cambridge, you cannot expect him to function fully by making him work for a *sogo shosha*. Because he will not be able to create a broad and useful communications network for himself with the Japanese personnel in the head office and branch offices in Japan as well as those in the overseas offices. Without mastering the decision-making system of Japanese-style management as well as the pattern of the communication system that supports it, Westerners could not create a *sogo shosha* even if they wanted to. . . ." (*Nihon Keizai Shimbun,* "Keizai Kyoshitsu", April 25, 1978)

Chapter 5

ENVIRONMENTAL CHANGES

AND MANAGEMENT CLIMATE

5.1 DISSATISFACTION WITH HIGH GROWTH

5.1.1 Frustrations

Japanese-style management has been created as one variation of an adaptation formula as it responded to environmental challenges that each age and time offered and the entrepreneurs strove to implement management practices that conformed to the orientations of the Japanese. Thus, it can be regarded as having displayed efficiency in its own way (with the Japanese society at any rate).

What should be pointed out here is that the mere fact that Japanese-style management has been created to conform to and make full use of the Japanese people's orientation does not necessarily mean that it has been designed so that the desires of the Japanese materialize fully through their work life. The development of a Japanese-style management reflects the undivided effort to avoid methods that would generate great psychological resistance among the members in the process of attaining corporate objectives. At the same time, it reflects the intention to increase the dynamism of the organization by means of fully taking advantage of the psychological traits of the Japanese. Consequently, whereas the Japanese people may have found Japanese-style management easier to adapt than the American and European-style management, it always had the tendency to force people to turn their dissatisfactions — something that has always existed in Japanese organizations — inward within the organization.

As is often pointed out, Japanese-style management, which displayed its strength during the high economic growth period, started revealing its weaknesses as we moved into the period of low growth. Before going into these weaknesses, it is necessary to study the dissatisfaction with the management system, which started unveiling even during the high growth period. This can be very useful in evaluating the counter-measures to be taken for solving various contradictions that have surfaced in this age of low growth.

In the foregoing chapters, I have presented studies on the efficiency of Japanese-style management and the many factors supporting it. The fact is that these same factors forced the organization members to keep in their frustrations and dissatisfactions. Since, during the high growth period, (1) it was easy to switch jobs due to labour shortage, and (2) it became relatively easy to *"de-salaryman-ize"* onself due to a favourable business climate, the dissatisfactions led to a number of people leaving the company for another opportunity. This sort of action requires a major decisions under the Japanese management system in which the permanence of relations is a fundamental principle. It is worth noticing that even within Japanese organizations, there exist dissatisfaction strong enough to force people to take that bold step.

The dissatisfactions exploded in the form of concrete actions when environmental pressure relaxed under high economic growth. This phenomenon could be regarded as a challenge against Japanese-style management. Nevertheless, many companies were too busy with their expansion and could not spare the time to respond to such a challenge and review their systems. Thus, no countermeasures were designed.

With the oil shock of 1973 as the turning point, all of a sudden the Japanese economy entered a recession and we can still expect the low growth period to continue for quite a long time. Under such circumstantial changes, people working for various organizations have again started seeking "stability" and "security" and the move towards leaving companies slowed down. Stories are heard about people who left their organizations during the high growth period and are now having a hard time. Those who stayed on are showing signs of relief at not having jumped the gun. But this does not mean that the essence of Japanese-style management has changed or that the problems faced by Japanese organizations have been solved. In the following sections, we shall study the structure of dissatisfactions created within Japanese companies and how they "turn inward".

5.1.2 The Mechanism of Dissatisfaction

I have already made it clear that the maintenance of a permanent relationship and the creation and maintenance of a harmonious and conformable relationship are the major prerequisites of Japanese-style management. These principles guarantee status security for the organization members and offer justifications for members to unite their forces for the attainment of the organization objectives. It also makes it possible for Japanese companies to display their strength fully as a body and played an important role in making companies a relatively comfortable place to live.

The fact that the maintenance of a permanent relationship as well as the creation and maintenance of a harmonious and conformable relationship easily struck roots among the Japanese signifies that within the Japanese mentality there is a kind of natural affinity for such relationships. The reactions of the members towards systems that aim to maintain such relationships are quite different in the United States and Europe, as well as in many Asian countries. Such differences in the reactions are obvious when we look at how the people react to measures taken by companies to include their members to stay on. Let us study an explanation offered by Vance Packard. He describes such measures taken by American companies as follows.

He says a corporate executive's loyalty towards the company is reinforced by the deferred payment of his remuneration, a measure designed by the company to hold onto him. Packard explains that since the executive is bound to the company in terms of remuneration, he would be losing a great amount of salary he had accumulated, and is with-held by the company, if he decides to quit halfway through his contract. He also goes on to point out that this measure of deferred reward is designed to make the executive possess a constant fear of losing his job and consequently prevents him from making disadvantageous moves such as clashing head-on with the decisions of top management. (*The Pyramid Climbers*, translated into Japanese by Tokuyama and Hara and published in Japan under the title, *Piramiddo wo Noboru Hitobito*, p. 12)

After this explanation, Packard introduces an example of an executive who claims that this system exerts an unbelievably heavy pressure when one tries to be honest, and expresses his doubt as to whether such inhuman control is really necessary or not (ibid.)

This argument by Packard seems to suggest two very interesting points. First is the fact that in the United States, this kind of a measure to prevent people from leaving the company is regarded as heavy pressure on a man's honesty. Secondly, deferred payment of remuneration is regarded as an inhuman control in the United States and thus people resist it strongly.

On the other hand, the reactions of the Japanese towards similar measures are quite different from those of the Americans. With regard to the age-grade pay system and severance pay scheme, both a form of "deferred payments of remunerations", the Japanese: (1) do not usually consider them a pressure on a "man's honesty"; and (2) do not show strong resistance to such deferred payments of remuneration but rather tend to be more concerned about the low amount of severance pay. For example, one often hears gripe like, "Your whole severance pay is gone after you buy a modest house!" This illustrates the mentality of the Japanese, that the larger the deferred payment is, the more assured one feels. Such differences in reaction between the Americans and the Japanese reflect: (1) the differences in the means of handling the tension between the group and the individual; and (2) the differences in the concept of the individual-group relationship.

First of all, for a Japanese, the tension between the group and the individual is basically dealt with by means of separating *tatemae* (one's official stance) and *honne* (one's true intentions). As for the various relations within a group, things are kept on the *tatemae* level when that is regarded as appropriate, and on the *honne* level if the individual is hid discreetly within. As a result, harmonious or conformable relations are maintained within the group.

On the other hand, the *honne* which each individual has kept locked up within himself explodes as dissatisfaction over a drink with intimate friends with whom he enjoys an "unconstrained" relationship. Sometimes, it can explode on occasions such as a company party. However, as long as the statements or actions do not seriously rock the boat of conformity in the day-to-day relations within the group, this is generally tolerated. What is interesting is that anyone who tries to make an issue of such behaviour shown during a drinking party is liable to be criticized. This can perhaps lead us to an interpretation that in Japanese group life, conformity in day-to-day relations (which is a conformity based on *tatemae*) and drinking parties for letting out one's *honne* exist as "institutions", each · one complementing the other. A Japanese learns to distinguish *tatemae* from *honne,* or vice versa, as he grows from childhood into adulthood as a part of his social training. Takeo Dio, a psychiatrist, comments as follows on this point.

"*Tatemae* is a type of principle that allows harmony among the masses. ... The dissatisfactions that remain are tucked away as *honne.* It is not an exaggeration to say that this is the biggest lesson a child has to learn in becoming an adult. It often accompanies an extremely painful process. ... Eventually, he learns that this dual concept is something that is inevitable for living in society and soon finds himself skillfully manipulating the two concepts of *tatemae* and *honne.* At this point, he has become a fully grown man. ... " (*"Amae" Zakko* (Thoughts on "Amae"), pp. 77-8)

For a Japanese who has received this training since childhood, the act of expressing agreement or maintaining silence towards a decision coming from the top and with which he does not agree, is regarded as an expression of his "cooperativeness". The method of holding onto personnel by means of deferred payment of remuneration is, therefore, not felt as pressure on a person's "honesty" in most cases.

To the contrary, most Americans would regard such a separation of *tatemae* and *honne* as "dishonesty one should be ashamed of". Thus, the application of Japanese-style solution for the tension existing between an American individual and his group would be extremely difficult, if not impossible. An American would tend to resort to the following two means to cope with such tension: (1) to limit, as much as possible, his relations with the group both functionally and time-wise thus allowing him to participate with the group within the framework of the limited scope and preventing him from getting too deeply involved with a certain group; and (2) to work on the basis of voluntary participation with the group, i.e. to obtain the freedom to leave the group at any time.

Consequently, measures to induce workers to stay on with the company that obviously restrict this "freedom to leave" is seen as a heavy pressure on a person's "honesty" and also a very inhuman control that makes the treatment of the tension between the individual and the group even more difficult. Because of this situation, the recent reinforcement of measures to stop executives from leaving and the demand for high level loyalty that imply some sacrifice of the workers' personal life have created a serious conflict with the ideology of "independence" deeply rooted among the Americans.

It must be realized, however, that although the Japanese-style solution of distinguishing between *tatemae* and *honne* does relax the tension between the individual and the group by means of creating a conformable relationship, it also forces the unappeased dissatisfactions within one's *honne* to turn keenly inward within the level of individual psychology. The words spit out by many salaried employees illustrate this very vividly: "You ask me if work at the office is interesting? How on earth could it be! If working were such a pleasant experience, there would not be so many bars and pubs doing such good business."

This type of pressure exists in Japan because the group structure is adopted among the Japanese companies. Similar pressures are not ordinarily detected among American and European-type organizations. In American and European organizations, individual tasks are clearly defined and the most important thing is to perform these tasks. Compared to Japanese companies, it is very seldom that group pressure is felt strongly in one's work place. To the contrary, in a Japanese company, the priority is to perform the job allocated to each work unit (as a section or a department) and to do so on the basis of concerted cooperation of the whole *group*. In so doing, individual circumstances are often ignored and it is demanded of the members to cooperate for the good of the group. In this sense, the tension between the group and the individual which has to be dealt with exists even more strongly in Japanese companies. Most of the time, the members somehow manage to deal with this problem by separating *honne* from *tatemae*. Thus, Japanese company members who on the surface *seem* to act in harmony and cooperatively may, under certain circumstance, be turning their dissatisfactions inward. And, the various systems designed to maintain permanent relations help keep such dissatisfactions from surfacing.

5.1.3 Dissatisfactions about Treatment

The biggest type of dissatisfaction that arises within Japanese companies is the question of treatment. As has been analyzed, we could detect a unique and strong sense of egalitarianism among the Japanese workers who are incredibly indifferent towards inequality in work burdens but who are highly sensitive about wage and other treatment differentials. This mentality is particularly noticeable in the post-war Japanese society where strict social status has been largely removed. This egalitarianism works together with the unique group awareness – supported by the sense of affiliation – to direct the interest of people mainly towards and within the group. Concern towards the world outside the group one is affiliated with is very limited. As a result, their awareness of status becomes very unique as well.

The awareness of a Japanese regarding status tends to be directed towards the social prestige of the group and one's status within that group. Thus, a Japanese will show indifference or dull concern to treatment differentials between his own organization and that of another organization but will show a sharp reaction towards the slightest treatment differentials within his own organization. In addition, since the concept of capabilities is such among the Japanese people that the evaluation of a person's capabilities is easily linked together with the evaluation of that person as a human being, this tendency is further accelerated. The slightest differences in treatment would bring about tremendous dissatisfaction among the Japanese while their sensitivity towards evaluation controls their "self" to a more than necessary degree and forces them to "silently" accept the demands of the organization.

For example, when a Japanese is ordered to handle a special assignment that requires him to work outside of his regular working hours and on a day for which he had planned something important for himself, he would rarely object to it by explaining his situation. Even when that assignment can be handled by someone else, he would most likely accept it in silence. Because of this custom, the greatest care must be taken with regard to treatment in a Japanese organization. The least mistake in dealing with this issue could bring about great dissatisfaction within the organization and such dissatisfaction could turn inward towards the organization in many undesirable forms. Very often, such dissatisfaction comes out in a deformed shape and creates unsound human relations or serves as a big psychological obstacle against effective labour participation.

Although it is a bit embarrassing, I shall draw upon a personal experience of mine concerning this point. This is when I was a salaried worker and I turned my dissatisfaction, created by some troubles with my boss, inward. I was ordered to prepare a chart that could ordinarily be done in about 15 minutes. Having been humiliated by my boss, I goofed a couple of times and finally completed the chart after two hours. The chart was not the most beautiful work either. It was not as if I were being lazy. As far as I was concerned, I was working like the dickens during those two hours. Perhaps, I was unconsciously pushing myself with an obsession or fantasies were going through my mind. This kind of an attitude obviously invites a scolding from the boss. When scolded, do people feel sorry about their stupidity? To the contrary, they will probably just stare straight into the boss' eyes, driven by a hatred that makes them want to leave the room and slam the door behind them. That was the way I felt. In this case, I was probably the one to be blamed. But so long as the system is such that a person cannot be fired, it is wisest to avoid such a scene by all means. Even if you openly label someone an "incompetent", that is not going to increase the dynamism of the organization. In fact, it will only be a drag on the organization.

In connection with the problem of the shortage of mangerial posts, there is much talk recently about the introduction of the merit system (as opposed to the seniority-oriented age-grade system) and reinforcement of a capability-oriented pay system. These suggestions that come from management "analysists" and elite businessmen are based on elitist ideas and may provide them with a feeling of pleasure but it is doubtful if they can contribute in any significant way to Japanese companies. Their suggestions would only increase the "difficulties and unpleasantness of working" in Japanese companies and reinforce the tendency of turning dissatisfactions inward.

5.2 CONTRADICTIONS REVEALED BY LOW GROWTH
5.2.1 Problems of the "Bloated" Structure

Traditionally, importance has been attached to the age structure in Japanese companies. Even when the organization was rapidly expanding, adding necessary personnel all at once at all levels was avoided. Instead, the method of gradually expanding recruitment, while taking into consideration the overall age structure of the company, was commonly practised. In bad times as well, even when there was surplus personnel, a certain number of freshmen have been hired during every recruitment season to fill the possible needs in the future. This idea of stressing the age structure derives from the seniority concept recognized in Japanese-style management. And, in that Japanese companies were structured and founded on such a concept, maintaining a proper age balance was a necessary consideration for the system to function smoothly.

This is also clear from the fact that with the coming of the low economic growth age, distortions started appearing in the age structure of Japanese companies and this led to an incredible number of problems that will be discussed later. Japanese companies had developed under this concept of attaching value to the age structure of the organization. This approach prevents the organizations from hiring personnel based on the current needs but encourages them to forecast the size of personnel needed in the future and hire people on the basis of that forecast and in consideration of the overall age structure. This tendency was accelerated during the high growth period of the Japanese economy when companies showed an almost "frantic" enthusiasm towards expansion and forecasted never-ending growth. More and more people were hired based on the forecasts for continued high economic growth.

The other factor that accelerated this tendency was the unique nature of Japanese-style competition among companies. This phenomenon was recognized during many postwar phases but was particularly strong during this period. Rather than choosing to improve investment returns by rationalizing business activities, many companies opted for mass introduction of funds from outside sources to attain rapid growth, expansion of the corporate scale and market share, higher evaluation and ranking in the industry, and a rise in social prestige.* As Koji Kobayashi put it, whereas an American company is a commercial undertaking, a Japanese company was looked upon as a "castle".

Thus, the effort to raise the company's prestige was first directed towards sales. That the ranking of life insurance companies was based not on the volume of assets held but on the volume of contracts is a reflection of such a competition. (Recently, with the coming of the low growth era, the system was changed to ranking by assets.) This kind of competition brought about a vigorous sales race using "human wave tactice", a method that ignored efficiency. As a result, one of the major concerns of the companies during the high growth period was to increase staff. Masumi

---

* It cannot be denied that the status awareness of the Japanese, which attaches value to the social prestige of the group one is affiliated with, was one of the major factors for this tendency. We must also bear in mind that it is this same concept that provided Japanese companies with a lively dynamism.

Tsuda comments as follows regarding this point.

"The scale of recruitment of newly graduated people, especially of university graduates, was unbelievably massive in March 1974. This massive hiring was probably brought about by the fact that the oil shock was not forseen at that stage, and Japan had been experiencing high growth ever since it overcame the recession in 1965. In those days, the name of the game was quantity, not quality. So the personnel department was forced to frantically hire people, posing many difficulties for the department." (*Nihon Keizai Kenkyu Center Bulletin*, No. 322, p. 39)

With the coming of the post-oil shock long-term recession, and in an age where we can expect low growth or so called stable growth to continue over an extended period of time, Japanese companies that went around hiring people right and left have begun to feel the sharp edges of their bloated structure.

5.2.2 Changes in the Age Structure and Aging of Organizations

As Japan's economy faced the long-term recession triggered by the oil shock in 1973, even the growth-conscious Japanese companies started to notice their bloated structure. Thus, under the slogan of "weight reduction management", many companies started reducing the number of new recruits fresh from school. As a result, the pyramid-shaped age structure started crumbling and it is common knowledge that many problems surfaced at this point.

More concretely, many companies now realize that if things kept on going this way, one day they would not be able to bear the burden of massive severance pay, that as the average age of the workers gets higher, the average wage goes up more too under the age-grade pay scheme, that the corporate vitality may slacken due to the aging of the members, and that there is an increasing shortage of managerial posts as more and more old-timers become eligible (by age and years of service) for those positions. All of these are extremely serious problems that have to be solved. They are not merely problems of corporate recruitment policies but imply efforts at coping with the fundamental issue of Japan's aging society which will generate even more aged workers in the future. (See Figure 5.1 for the age structure of the working population.)

Because of this change in the age structure, the problem of a shortage of managerial posts will become an even graver issue in the future. According to the "Survey on Promotions" conducted by Nippon Recruit Center in April 1978, already at that time, 61.4% of all companies surveyed were experiencing a slower pace of promotions as compared to the high growth period. In particular, the figure was as high as 70% for the category of companies with 1,000 or more employees. Although the delay was only by one year as compared with the survey conducted in September 1974, this slowing down of promotion pace is expected to continue in the future unless a screening method for managerial posts were introduced rapidly. At any rate, it is bound to affect the work morale of the members of the company greatly. The same survey also shows that 44.5% of the companies had carried out some sort of reform in their promotion system during the previous three years, and 29.6% of the companies were planning to do so in the near future. Thus, a total of 74.1% of the companies were involved in reforms, the contents of which would probably include "establishment or revision of the personnel evaluation system", "creation or expansion of the specialists' post", and "introduction of a new performance evaluation system".

Source: Nihon Keizai Shimbun, April 16, 1977.

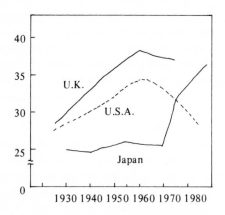

Figure 5.1   Share of Those in the 45-64 Years Old Age Bracket among Male Workers Aged 15-64

If these issues can be regarded merely as a question of management techniques, the whole matter would be very simple (See Chapter I). That is to say, the problems of the bloated structure become a major issue because this clashes with the lifetime employment system, and the various problems arising from the "age structure distortion" are difficult to solve because they have to be studied within the context of the age-grade pay scheme. So, these problems should be easy to solve if we could just abolish the systems of life-time employment and age-grade pay. What is interesting is the fact that these problems that would be easily solved if one could resort to such means are actually proving to be big headaches for the employers and top management.

It is at this point that we encounter an important fact that was obvious to many entrepreneurs with any brains but that the economists and analysts of business management, who simple-mindedly promoted American-style management, have constantly overlooked. And that fact is that a management system is not something that can be forced upon the employees by management. Because of this fact, it is necessary to understand management as a system, not merely as a question of techniques. This has already been explained in Chapter 1.

5.3   ENVIRONMENTAL CHANGES

In Chapter 3, the following three conditions were mentioned as factors preventing quick responses to environmental changes. First, once a certain management system has penetrated widely throughout a society, the very fact that the system tries to strike firm roots in that society forces the system to display a strong constraining force. Secondly, each management system is a part of the overall institution, i.e. it functions together with various other management systems and formulas to form an overall "conglomerate" of systems. For this reason, revision of one system would have various impact on other areas of the overall institution.

In particular, since Japanese-style management was created with the idea of permanent relations as the basic concept for the core workforce, lifetime employment and age-grade pay serve as the basic framework of the overall system. All other systems within Japanese management are formed on the basis of this framework. Thus, any revision thereof can be assumed to have an extremely great influence on the overall institution of Japanese management. It was also trigger a not inconsiderable resistance from the other areas of the management system.

Thirdly, some of the management systems are closely linked with the psychology encountered widely among the members of the society. This is noticeably so when the system deals with human affairs, in particular with questions concerning the members' status. Therefore, in some cases, the revision of such a system would be met with great psychological resistance from the people. This sort of psychological resistance is different in nature from the perplexity accompanying a simple transfer of systems which is basically a feeling of confusion arising from unfamiliarity with the situation. It can have a pervasive impact on the formation process of a system.

These three factors will be dealt with in detail in the following sections.

5.3.1 Constraining Force Displayed by Established Management Systems

Basically, a management system is something that each company tries to create and maintain as a tool to respond to environmental changes and attain its business objectives. So, it ends up being a conglomerate of various management formulas, each with characteristic features reflecting the history and varied environmental conditions surrounding the company as well as the unique circumstances of the corporate body. But, at the same time, as we already mentioned, since the top management's concept of man and reactions of the corporate members, both of which exert great influence on the formation process of a management system (the latter through the form of "feedback"), are based on the unique psychological foundations that have been created on a common cultural basis, some of the management systems end up being widely established throughout the society. Therefore, this issue of the constraining force displayed by management systems that have struck roots in the society overlaps to some extent with the question of psychological foundations discussed in section 5.3.3. However, for a theoretical discussion, it can be taken up separately.

If a right-hand traffic system were implemented for just part of the road network in a society where left-hand traffic is already established, it would create various difficulties and would be highly dangerous. Therefore, the adoption of a partial right-hand traffic rule would be nearly impossible. When I was in the United States, I heard of the story of an old British lady who was stopped by the police because she was speeding along the left-hand side of the highway. My American friend who told me this story seemed to think that this lady was already senile to do such a thing. I have also experienced this during a car ride in the United States, with a Japanese lady as the driver, when she tried to go into the left lane as she made a turn at a crossing. Although this lady had lived in the United States for some time, the fact that the car was packed with her Japanese friends and she was absorbed in a conversation in Japanese seems to have made her recall her driving habits back in Japan. In an ever-shrinking world, differences in systems can create frictions even when dealing in two different societies.

In Japanese society, various systems including lifetime employment and the age-grade pay scheme have penetrated widely. A type of constraining power can be assumed to exist within these systems just as in the case of the left-hand traffic system. That is to say, in an environment where life-time employment has struck roots, it is extremely difficult for just a handful of companies to disregard this system. In a society like this, most of the major companies hire newly graduated people every April and keep most of them until they reach retirement age. Hiring of people outside this recruitment season and half way through the career ladder does exist, but they are still regarded as "exceptional cases". This means that as far as the workers are concerned, once you leave a company, your chances of finding a decent job elsewhere is very limited.

Let us assume that some companies abolished the life-time employment system despite the prevailing circumstances. Would the workers be willing to choose a company that offered slightly better conditions but in which there was a high possibility of being dismissed? If the younger generation is seeking security (as seems to be the recent trend) and keeps opting for companies where lifetime employment is practised, these "progressive" companies would encounter difficulties in recruiting people and may end up accepting people who were not good enough to land on any other jobs. Furthermore, when they dismiss their own employees and try to find people to fill the vacancy — which of course signifies a "mid-career" recruitment — the scope of selection will be quite limited. If it is difficult to hire people midway through their career, the alternative is to train people you already have. So, it is rather obvious that in a society where the lifetime employment system is established, it is exceedingly difficult, aside from companies in very unique positions, for just a part of the companies to try to abolish the system.

The same can be said for the scheduled annual recruitment practice for new graduates* and for the attempt at introducing the Western-style merit system. When the companies compete against each other to obtain good material from the lot of new graduates and hire them in a batch every April it is extremely difficult for a few companies to adopt a different recruitment method. The open secret of the breach of the recruitment agreement** just goes to show what kind of priority most companies place on the race in this annual recruitment campaign for new graduates and is just one sign of how difficult it will be to resort to a different system.

The same sort of factors exist for the introduction of the merit system. If the merit system were introduced into a Japanese organization where there is no escape exits under the lifetime employment system, it would most probably bring about the harshest conditions for the workers. If people who devoted a major portion of their life were to be evaluated by a unilateral yardstick by the management and have their

---

*   See footnote on page 52 of Chapter 3.

**   Despite the agreement between the Ministry of Labour and among the companies in Japan that recruitment campaigns for graduates-to-be not be initiated before October 1 (i.e. six months before graduation), many companies start their campaigns well before that in hope of getting good people.

life clearly labelled as a success or a failure, the impact would be tremendous and hardly bearable for these people. So, if most Japanese people still preferred the "capability-oriented" age-grade pay system,* companies adopting the merit system would be affected in the same way as in the case of abolishment of the lifetime employment system.

These few examples illustrate the idea that systems that have become widely accepted in a society often exercise strong constraining force. Needless to say, the impact of such a constraining force differs greatly from one system to another and it is also closely connected with the question of the psychological foundations of the systems as will be explained in Section 5.3.3. Thus, when a considerable number of companies do take the step of abolishing these systems because the psychological foundations have changed greatly or under strong environmental pressures, it signifies that the system is no longer socially established. In such a case, the constraining force will weaken. As the constraining force declines, more companies may decide to abolish the system. In this way, by the force of an "accelerated cycle", a system that once exercised strong constraining force can collapse rapidly and quite suddenly. This can be understood as an "antagonism" between the constraining force of an established system and the forces trying to destroy it.

5.3.2 Management Systems as a Conglomerate

The second conceivable factor that prevents the revision of management systems is the far-reaching effect that the revision of a single system may have over the total system of management. To illustrate this, let us take up the question of a higher retirement age, an issue that is much talked about recently.

(i)   Far-reaching Effect of a Higher Retirement Age

The age retirement system has been maintained by many Japanese companies as something very closely connected with lifetime employment and age-grade pay. It has not merely existed as a system to cope with a decline in the working capability of old workers. Rather, it has served as a kind of a safety value for Japanese-style management implemented under the framework of lifetime employment and age-grade pay. Thus, there has been a tendency, especially after the Second World War, for this system to be applied completely separately from the idea of declining working capabilities.

Over recent years, not only has the average life expectancy of the Japanese expanded but the pace of aging has also slowed down. It is said

---

* See Chapter 2, Section 2.2.2.

that a 65-year old person today possesses the physical strength and intellectual capacity of a 50-year old some years back. In the case of a managerial or administrative officer, a decline in physical stamina does not affect his work performance that much. In fact, in the Japanese business environment, some of the most important qualities one must possess to carry out administrative tasks smoothly are to have abundant experience within the organization and be versed in the affairs of other sections and departments within the company, to have a thorough knowledge of the historical background of crucial corporate issues, and to have maintained friendly human relations with the members of the company as well as building up solid trust relationships with the subordinates. So, for many people in managerial posts, the mid-fifties is the peak of one's career. Nevertheless, for many years, the prescribed retirement age remained unchanged at 55 and it is only very recently that the adoption of a slightly higher retirement age is being slowly implemented under pressure from various circles.

Resistance to a higher retirement age is probably closely related to the question of lifetime employment and age-grade pay, in particular the latter. As far as management is concerned, since many of the companies are immersed in efforts to "reduce weight", a higher retirement age entails an adverse effect under the age-grade pay system. Moreover, since delaying the retirement age means fewer people recruited at the other end of the scale, it will contribute further to the distortion of the age structure which started appearing during the post-oil shock recession. It will accelerate the shortage of managerial posts and under the age-grade pay scheme the wage costs would increase imposing a heavier burden on the company. If the older people were to be deprived of titles, that would have a complicated effect on the junior-senior relationship among the Japanese and imply dealing with the issue of the psychological foundations of Japanese management, as will be discussed in 5.3.3. As can be seen from this example with the retirement system, the various systems of management are closely related to each other and thus a revision of one or just a few systems often clashes with, or at least greatly affects, the other areas of management.

(ii) The Basic Framework of Lifetime Employment

The same can be said of both lifetime employment and the age-grade pay systems. In particular, with regard to lifetime employment, as we explained in detail in Chapter 3, since it offers a framework for the institutional structure of Japanese management based on the permanence of relations, its abolishment carries the danger of shaking at the very root the faith that the workers and the staff memebers have towards the company. Not only that, it could destroy the present form of management completely to have a strong impact on every aspect. What we must be careful about here is that the phrase "collapse of the lifetime employment system" can be used to mean various things depending on the person using it and that entails the danger of creating misunderstandings.

One person may insist on the strict definition of the word "lifetime" and claim that under the current situation in which the retirement age is set at 55 and the average life expectancy has exceeded 70, there is no such thing as *lifetime* employment in Japan. This argument does make sense as long as you are just concerned with the semantics of the terminology. The argument is not exactly on the same level as the question of the collapse of the system. Indeed, the statement does carry some significance in that it points out that the current system no longer guarantees "lifetime" employment because there has been a drastic change in the conditions, namely that the average life expectancy of the Japanese has increased greatly. However, this particular change in conditions has not led to the collapse of the system that has functioned as a framework for the various management formulas that comprise Japanese-style management, a system based on long-term and stable relations. All one has to do is to read the words "lifetime employment system" as "long-term secured employment system". So if and when Japanese-style management will be affected down to its most essential elements by the abolishment of the lifetime employment system, this has to reflect the collapse of the system in the latter sense.

It is also possible to adopt a very rigid interpretation of "lifetime employment system" and regard as the collapse of the system such measures as soliciting for voluntary early retirement of the workers (as some companies have done under the pressure of the heavy burden of the long-term recession) or detaching a specific function of the company and founding a subsidiary (known as "spin-out") to which surplus older workers can be sent. Or, as Tsuda remarked, this spin-out phenomenon could be interpreted as the very "limit" what can still be considered as being within the framework of the lifetime employment system.

The concept of lifetime employment covers a different scope depending on its interpretation. I tend to adopt a rather loose interpretation of the term. I regard these taps-on-the-shoulder and spin-out measures as an effort to protect Japanese-style management in the main body, i.e. the parent company, in particular for its core workforce. I regard them as measures to protect lifetime employment by destroying just a small part of the lifetime employment system. Thus, I take the stance that when, within the core of a Japanese company, the members can anticipate "long-term secured employment" until the prescribed retirement age as long as the existence of the company is not put at stake, this can be referred to as lifetime employment or more appropriately "long-term secured employment". So long as the core segment of Japanese-style management carries a considerable weight, this interpretation can be regarded as being most appropriate in analyzing the tendencies of Japanese-style management which is created and maintained with the permanence of relations as the basic prerequisite.

(iii) Age-grade Pay System and the Metabolic Function

The same thing can be said for the age-grade pay system as for the lifetime employment system. As concerns the age-grade pay system, I tend to stress its connection with the psychological foundations of the Japanese which will be discussed in the following section. But it cannot be denied that its mutual relationship with the other systems of management have resulted in great resistance to its revision or abolishment. The age-grade pay system is closely connected with the systems of continual promotions and rotations. Consequently, through these systems, it is also closely related to the system of bringing up managers and supervisors among the in-house staff members known as "supervisorism". It has something to do with the group structure of Japanese organizations as well. It is further linked with the recruitment practices, personnel allocation methods, system of inter-departmental assistance, and the regular-staff system of Japanese companies. The age-grade pay system forms the framework of Japanese-style management, the framework that I refer to as the "metabolic function". For the readers' convenience, I shall describe this "metabolism" of Japanese companies.

When an undesired situation arises with regard to a part of an American or a European organization, this segment can be dropped through dismissal and the organization is regenerated by hiring necessary people anew. This is a method that could be likened to surgery. On the other hand, the regeneration of a Japanese company is accomplished by a method that could be compared to the metabolic functions of a living body. In order to regenerate the company while maintaining the age-grade (or seniority) principle which supports the status order in Japanese organizations as well as the principle of harmony among the members of the company, the age retirement system, under which the aged segment is dropped, is strictly observed while new school leavers are hired every year. Since graduation from school takes place every March, the hiring of new graduates take the form of annual recruitment. The batch of new employees joining the companies every April theoretically climbs the career ladder, created on the basis of the seniority principle, step by step each year. These members go through the process of continual promotions, each level being only slightly higher than the one before, and continue to do so until they reach the prescribed retirement age. Because of the existence of this system, the age structure (or more precisely, the age-grade structure) of all the organization members is looked upon as something quite important in Japanese organizations. Thus, people are taken in not only on the basis of operational needs but sometimes because there is a need to do so from an age-structure point of view. By hiring extra personnel in this way, there is always some flexibility in the allocation of staff, enabling on-the-job training and offering overall flexibility to the organization as a whole.

With the working lifespan of people as "one cycle", i.e. from the moment they appear on the labour market until they retire (by age), a metabolic regeneration of organizations is constantly being carried out in extremely long-term cycles. And because the age structure of the organization is so important, recruitment plans are drawn up every year based on the long-term forecast of people who will retire due to age and any expected expansion of work. This method is not only designed to cope with the aging segment of the organization, it also copes flexibly with the various factors that affect order within companies, e.g. expansion of work due to environmental changes, vacancies in important posts, and necessity of performance evaluation. It is an excellent framework conforming to the formation principles of Japanese-style management, i.e. to introduce changes slowly into the organization, avoiding any abrupt changes. For instance, to cope with organizational expansion during the high growth period, the Japanese companies tended to acquire the necessary manpower by gradually increasing the "intake" in this metabolic cycle rather than by resorting to the method of hiring people at different levels directly from the labour market which would have greatly disturbed the in-house order. As a result, the expansion of organizations was achieved without drastically destroying the age structure and age-grade principle within the organizations. Because of this method of expansion, the size of the staff grew considerably but the status order within the company was protected from any extreme changes. Even when a vacancy occurring for an important post was filled, that did not have serious repercussions on the members, excepting perhaps for the few corporate officers directly involved, as it would commonly have in the United States. This is because, due to the continual promotion system, those who did not make it this time were more or less guaranteed to eventually end up in similar posts. To the contrary, in an American company, as Packard points out, the fact that a vacancy is filled brings about great disappointments and dissatisfactions within the organization.

As the three examples of a higher retirement age, lifetime employment, and age-grade pay illustrate, the management systems are closely related to each other and the revision and/or abolishment of any systems, in particular the basic ones that form the framework, seriously affect the overall style of management. Therefore, this can become one of the obstacles when an attempt is made to change any management system in response to sudden fluctuations in the environment.

5.3.3 Conflict with the Psychological Foundations

The style of Japanese management is deeply linked, in many respects, with the group orientation of the Japanese as well as with the various characteristics arising out of this group mentality, i.e. the awareness of *uchi* (inside) and *soto* (outside), tendency to assimilate with the group, and the Japanese concept of status and responsibility. The relationship between these psychological foundations and Japanese-style management will be discussed in detail in Chapter 6. In this section, studies will be made regarding the conflict between psychological foundations and revision and/or abolishment of the age-grade pay system.

While an American or a European will try to limit his relations with a group functionally and time-wise, a Japanese will build an affiliation awareness towards a certain group, will relate to the group in a number of ways, and have an emotional feeling of "oneness" with the group. At the same time, his concern towards the world outside this particular group tends to become very weak. As a result, a Japanese person's awareness of his status is felt not so much in terms of how it compares with the people outside the group but rather how it compares with the other members within the same organization. Moreover, for the Japanese who devote the major portion of their active working life to the group under the long-term employment practice, this question of whether they gain a satisfactory status within the group or not is an highly important issue, as important as determining the success or failure of one's life.

The unique egalitarianism of the Japanese, i.e. the tendency of being quite indifferent about fairness in work sharing but being excessively sensitive about wage and other treatment differentials, is closely connected with this question of status awareness. In the modern age in which the strict status awareness and master-servant relationships that were predominant in the pre-war Japanese society have been swept away and when most Japanese possess a middle-class consciousness, this concept of egalitarianism tends to show up in even wider contexts. Of course, it is possible to look at it the other way around, too. That the wage system based on age-grade prevented the widening of the income gaps, created a mass of middle-class population, and supported the high growth of an economy based on mass-production and mass-consumption. In any event, we cannot deny the fact that now that we have created such a society, the forementioned type of egalitarianism will be even more noticeable.

Under these circumstances, the conventional method of introducing slight differentials under the system of continual promotion can be said to have been very conformable to the psychological foundations to Japanese-style management. Indeed, that is the reason it has brought about many fruitful results. To deal with the Japanese organization members who are extremely sensitive about wage and treatment differentials, the gradual introduction of very small differentials was practised to give them time to get used to the gaps while eventually granting the appropriate posts to those with the capability to fill them. This formula not only had the advantage of dampening the impact while still attaining the objectives but also offered opportunities of participation in the race for promotion to most of the members. Furthermore, by keeping as many members as possible in the competition for maximum periods of time, a kind of dynamism that cannot be found in Western organizations was developed within Japanese companies. And this method of offering only minimal differentials kept the incentive scheme very economical. Needless to say, it also helped narrow the income gaps among the Japanese workers and contributed to the creation of a stable society.

So, the age-grade pay system, which has often been the target of criticism, has actually displayed some excellent functions. At the same time, we must realize that since it is very closely connected with the psychological foundations of Japanese-style management, the resistance from the psychological foundations has made any hasty revision of the system difficult.

We have so far proven that the revision of management systems often faces strong resistance because of factors such as: (1) the constraining force exerted by any system that has been socially established; (2) the far-reaching effect that the revision is likely to have on the overall system; and, (3) the conflict with the psychological foundations. But, as already mentioned, even the constraining force of a socially established system can decline rapidly once it starts to collapse. With regard to the question of impact on the overall system, as the environmental requirements for the revision of a system grow stronger, changes can be gradually introduced while coordination is established concerning the possible repercussions on other areas of the overall system. Even the psychological foundations, which are considered extremely resistant to changes, are not totally immune to changes. An explanation of this point has already been made. (*Nihon Keizai Shimbun,* March 3, 1978) The thrust of the explanation is as follows.

It can be assumed that most of the reasonable entrepreneurs in the past had formed their management systems taking into full consideration the mentalities of the workers. Today, they are suffering from being "sandwiched" between the drastic environmental changes triggered by the oil crisis and the national psychological traits deeply imbedded among the Japanese people. Some companies, faced with the serious recession and finding no other way out are starting to experiment with the introduction of a "merit system" into their basically Japanese-style management.

The outcome of these experiments is not yet clear. It may create a higher work morale within the companies, it may create a large "drift" of dropouts who choose to say, "Why bother?" and stop trying. If most of the younger generation preferred to stay away from the merit system, these companies may find difficulties in recruiting personnel. Or, to the contrary, they may end up getting the few who are full of eagerness and create a "crack unit". We still do not know how the younger generation, whose awareness is said to be changing, will support or resist these movements by the companies.

If more and more companies adopted merit system practices, and if the significance of college diplomas should start declining, the school system as well as home education would be greatly influenced. Consequently, significant changes may occur in the psychological traits and behavioural patterns of the Japanese. We can expect these kinds of dynamic relations between the national psychological traits and management systems to be manifested more often in the future, in many interesting ways. Here lies one of the central issues that the science of management in Japan has to focus on in the future.

What the science of management has to do is neither to introduce existing theories from abroad nor to try to adhere persistently to the traditional Japanese practices. What it has to do is to clarify the dynamic relations between the national psychological traits and the management systems.

Koji Kobayashi, Chairman of NEC, gave the following reply to my question of, "Under the lifetime employment system where there is no escape exit, would the introduction of a Western-type merit system, which hardly puts any emphasis on age or seniority, not create very harsh conditions?"

"That is a relative question. You can regulate the degree of action according to the reactions you get. We cannot suggest that the status quo should be maintained. A company has to survive by its own strive. With this cycle of action and reaction, it may take quite a long time but changes will occur slowly."

And, to the question of "Does that mean that the corporate executives should sometimes tighten the reins and at other times relax the reins?" Kobayashi replied, "No. Rather, gradual changes in the awareness of both the labour and management are necessary. There should be an atmosphere created among the union members to accept, to some extent, these changes." (*Nihon Keizai Kenkyu Center Bulletin,* No. 322, p. 44)

These adjustments represent the feeback of the employees' reactions in the formation process of management systems as touched upon in Chapter I and also the dynamic action-reaction relations between the rank-and-file members' awareness and management systems. I believe that through such adjustments and reforms implemented slowly and steadily by many entrepreneurs, management systems that will conform to the psychological foundations of the people and that can better respond to the environmental challenges will be developed. And, those systems that will have survived the subsequent "screening" process will eventually strike roots in the society.

Because of the existence of these various factors, although the revision of management systems is often possible on a long-term basis, it is difficult to expect them to react promptly to environmental changes. Nevertheless, the rapid environmental changes following the oil shock are forcing the corporate managers react quickly. This demand arising out of environmental changes, i.e. the need for a short-term response and its difficulty, together with the fact that although long-term revisions are possible the orientation is still very difficult to grasp, has created confusion among the top management and this indeed is the core of the problem that many corporate managers are confronting today. Chapter 6 will deal with the orientation of the long-term countermeasures.

Chapter 6
THE FUTURE OF JAPANESE-
STYLE MANAGEMENT

6.1 INTRODUCTION

I have consistently emphasized that Japanese-style management is a consequence of reforms entrepreneurs have undertaken over the years by anticipating the workers' reactions and/or by responding to the feedback coming from them. That is to say, Japanese-style management is the result of a choice by both management and labour. By the same token, new solutions to the various problems that Japanese-style management is currently facing will most likely be found through the painstaking efforts of the employers as they seek appropriate means.

Obviously, subjective and environmental conditions surrounding each company and the ways corporate managers perceive these issues vary, making their countermeasures rather diverse as well. It is expected, however, that these diverse countermeasures will have to go through a screening process, as illustrated in Figure 1-2 of Chapter I, and those that "survive" will eventually be brought together and reshaped into something even more conformable to reality. The remarks of Yajiro Ikari, President of Daimaru, Inc., (a large department store chain) concerning this point are very suggestive.

"In times as turbulent as ours, I believe that the top management, as well as those in other supervisory posts, should take another look at the front line of business (i.e. the "floor level" or field activities) and observe the realities of those actually working up there in the front line and of the work being accomplished by them. It is from these observations of reality that a new organization or a new work mechanism must be created. ... There is a saying that goes, 'An idea devised in motion is a million times more effective than one worked out while static.' These words signify that ideas created while one is moving, i.e. ideas generated from the shop floor and field, are a million times more effective than those worked out on paper at a desk. I believe that at this moment it is necessary for each and every member of the top management to fully appreciate the meaning of these words as a guideline adapted to current reality. . . ." (*Keiei to Hito* (Management and Man), Osaka Kogyo-kai & Kansai Productivity Center, pp. 147-8)

Considering that such remarks come from an entrepreneur who has carefully watched over and observed his company at the front line of management for many years, it is certainly most difficult for academic analysts of business management, who tend to lack first-hand experience of the challenges of the business world, to identify the future direction of Japanese-style management.

Recently, a number of reports have appeared that offer elaborate analyses of these issues.* Although these reports tend to be somewhat generalized, they do offer a broad outlook and types of conceivable countermeasures. In this chapter, I would like to present a brief description of my views concerning the future of lifetime employment and age-grade pay systems, from the viewpoint of their relations with the psychological foundation of Japanese-style management. Although I do expect that effective solutions will ultimately emerge through the painstaking efforts of the top management or by those who are in the front line of corporate activities, I feel that the approach of studying the basic nature of these issues from a different level will be instructive in its own way.

6.2 DIFFICULTIES IN ABOLISHING LIFETIME EMPLOYMENT

6.2.1 Good Will and Willingness to Make Japanese Organizations Function

Now that the post-oil shock recession has led us into the age of low growth, Japanese companies that once went wild expanding while dreaming of never-ending growth have accomplished a 180-degree turn to make efforts at cutting down their size, commonly referred to as a "weight reduction" of the organizational structure and mechanism. The issue attracted a great deal of attention among the public and at one time became the favourite subject in the press as a sign of the collapse of the lifetime employment system. It was also regarded as a serious problem for the middle-aged and elderly workers threatened by pressure for "voluntary" early retirement.

However, looking over the progress of things to date, it seems that aside from some of the industries that suffered from a structural recession and has to resort to means of encouraging voluntary retirement among their

---

* Examples of such reports include *Korei-ka Jidai no Chingin, Koyo Seido* (Wage and Employment Systems in an Aging Society), March 1978, which is a report by the Technical Committee on Wage Systems under the Japan Productivity Center, and *Chukonenrei-ka ni Taishosuru Korekara no Jinji, Chingin, Koyo Taisaku* (Future Personnel, Wage, and Employment Measures in Response to the Aging of Society), a report by the Workshop on Labour-Management Relations, under the Kansai Productivity Center.

workers, most of the companies tightened their belt, withstood – painful though it was – the burden of surplus manpower, and slowly brought about a "weight reduction" while keeping away from drastic measures. Some of the outstanding enterprises are said to have succeeded in considerable "weight reduction" at a relatively early stage. This style of "weight reduction" management will probably continue to be discussed in the future, especially in connection with the growing problems of an aging population and the age-grade pay system.

In reply to the question of "When we reach the stage of no longer being able to guarantee lifetime employment and age-grade pay for the older workers who literally devoted their lives to the reconstruction of the post-war Japanese economy, will we still be able to maintain the overall system of Japanese management?" Koji Kobayashi commented as follows.

"I am saying that the systems of lifetime employment and age-grade pay will change, not that they will disappear. It is difficult to describe exactly how they will change. But, for one, I think there will be a lot of spin-outs (the phenomenon of a certain function of a company separating itself from the organization and becoming a separate entity). Companies cannot continue to sustain much of the middle bulge in their structures. So, they establish separate companies and feed the work out. In these new companies, new systems are devised to carry out the work. . . . This spin-out approach began some 15 years ago. Today, it is becoming more and more popular. . . ." (*Nihon Keizai Kenkyu Center Bulletin,* No. 322, p. 41)

This tendency to re-examine the lifetime employment system has come about not so much as a countermeasure against the "bloated" structure of companies but more likely as a measure to cope with elderly workers, a means to rectify the distortion in the age structure of the workforce. So it is not as if the fundamentals of Japanese-style management were being questioned. Such painstaking measures would not be necessary if the parent company were free to drop the system of lifetime employment. What we are seeing should be regarded perhaps as an effort to maintain lifetime employment by partially revising the lifetime employment system itself. In fact, most Japanese companies, even when they find themselves amidst difficulties in the process of "weight reduction" or of rectifying the age structure, have avoided resorting to "surgical" methods as long as they could possibly resist this and concentrated their efforts on "weight reduction" through the "metabolic function" approaches.

This kind of behaviour by the Japanese companies must have come partially from human considerations regarding their workers. As we already mentioned, members of any Japanese organization are generally looked upon as buddies and colleagues working together, not as mere "replaceable parts". But this is not to say that such behaviour of the companies was supported only by human considerations. There must have been other factors taken into account such as preserving the corporate image, relations with the union, etc. On the more fundamental level, it derived from the fact that abolishing the lifetime employment system, a basic framework of Japanese-style management, was simply extremely difficult.

Studies were made in Chapter 5 on the three factors that hinder the abolishment of management systems. Lifetime employment is one of the management systems where these conditions fit in perfectly. It is a system against which the constraining forces that socially established systems display are exerted most effectively. This can be said in terms of the need for acquiring personnel. Thus, under the present circumstances, aside from some unique cases, it is almost impossible for any company to abolish the lifetime employment system *totally,* although it may be conceivable to carry out a partial dismissal of employees at times of corporate crisis.

Secondly, as described in Chapter 3, Japanese-style management exists with the permanence of relations as one of its prerequisites. Various considerations are incorporated in the system to keep relations as harmonious as possible under such a permanent relationship. Such considerations are detected in every aspect of management systems, giving various characteristic features to the Japanese style of management. This nature of Japanese-style management is recognized to have created business organizations differing totally in style and nature from the machine-model type institutions of Western societies, so different and unique that they are sometimes referred to as being "artistic". To abolish the lifetime employment system which functions as a framework for Japanese organizations would signify shaking Japanese-style management to its very roots. Unless there is some certainty about a management system that could replace it and function more effectively, it is indeed difficult, if not impossible, aside from partial revisions, to abolish the system.

Thirdly, the lifetime employment system fits in nearly with the group-orientation of the Japanese supported by the affiliation awareness and "familiarity" relationship. This group-orientation endows Japan's companies with dynamism and mobility in many forms. Thus again, from this psychological viewpoint as well, the abolishment of lifetime employment would most probably meet with great resistance. Unlike American and European organizations that function on the basis of contracts and obligations, Japanese organizations are mobilized by the members' good will and their willingness to contribute. So, under the currently prevailing situation, it is very important to acquire a core workforce that functions well, i.e. a core supported by group-orientation and mobility. And the means that Japanese companies have resorted to in order to acquire such fine core workers is the system of lifetime employment. The destruction of the principles of long-term secured employment among the core workers would give rise to serious confusion.

There is a great danger of the occurrence of a situation such as described by Masumi Tsuda, i.e. "In fact, in a certain company, the 'tap-on-the-shoulder' type of pressure for early retirement has become so prevalent even on the managerial level that people are so worried they cannot concentrate on their work." He goes on to conclude thus, "Lifetime employment practices should not be dropped."

As long as the companies adopt long-term secured employment policies, the creation of a flexible peripheral workforce that can absorb the shocks brought about by environmental fluctuations is necessary together with the acquisition of an outstanding core workforce. As far as I can tell, what we will see in the near future is not an overall review of the lifetime employment system but rather a move towards maintaining lifetime employment practices for the core workforce, thus sustaining its mobility, and more efforts at the creation of a periphery large enough to absorb shocks.

As shown by the analysis in Chapter 3, Japanese-style management has traditionally possessed this dual structure comprising a core and a periphery. Although there has been an expansion or shrinking of both portions at different times in history, the basic form of this structure has been maintained to date. Depending on how one looks at it, American and European organizations can be seen as institutions where a handful of top executives comprise the core while in Japanese companies, the core has been gradually expanding with time.

6.2.2 Means to Avoid Sudden Changes

Theoretically, there are many conceivable methods for absorbing the shocks generated by changes in the environment. For example, there is the method of resorting to routine overtime for processing work during busy seasons and doing away with such overtime during lean periods. There is also the method of laying off workers according to the amount of business activity. Another means is to maintain the dual structure of the workforce consisting of the core and the periphery as mentioned earlier. In view of management's relations with the union as well as of the various issues the Japanese companies face today, e.g. the increasing burden of severance pay due to the aging workforce, an increase in the average wage, and the lack of enough managerial posts to go around, the most acceptable future approach seems to be to maintain a versatile and flexible peripheral workforce.

It has already been mentioned that the unmarried female population had been the biggest source of such a periphery in the past. Until quite recently, this segment of the workforce consisted mainly of female high school graduates. More recently, some companies have expanded the scope to include female college graduates, attracting attention in the business community. The personnel management policies of Jusco, Ltd., a large supermarket chain, introduced in *Nikkei Business,* is a typical example of this.

"Jusco has already become known for its rapid growth brought about by its 'federal' management formula. Again, it has become a topic of interest with its extensive hiring of female college graduates. Obviously, this was the decision made by Ms. Kojima, who is currently the company's auditor. In 1978, the company took on a total of 357 female college graduates, most of them junior college graduates but also including as many as 102 four-year university graduates who are often ignored by companies. In the same industry, Nichii hired 61 women from junior colleges and universities and Ito Yokado 67. Jusco's figure of 357 is truly amazing. The company is almost like a savior for many university graduate females who are especially discriminated against on the recruitment front amidst the prevailing "weight reduction" atmosphere. Ms. Kojima claims that the decision came not out of sympathy for them or because she is a woman herself. It came from the mind of a strict businessperson. . . ." (*Nikkei Business,* July 31, 1978, p. 92)

What this "strict businessperson" intends to get is obviously a flexible periphery. Ms. Kojima clearly stated her intentions. "As long as the management is faced with the goal of cutting down the total personnel costs, you need a segment in your workforce that observes a certain cycle of turnover. The majority of the women you hire still regard as their future goal to quit working and become a housewife-mother. At the time of joining the company, there are no capability gaps between men and women. The massive recruitment of female college graduates is advantageous for both the company and the female workforce because it provides the former with good quality labour and offers the later an opportunity to train themselves in the world before retiring to their homes."

Behind this statement which clearly spells out the true intentions of the corporate management instead of trying to dress it up with pretty words lies a certain philosophy. That philosophy is summed up by Kojima, "It is up to the woman herself to decide whether as a woman she wants to attach more importance to her professional career or to bringing up children. The only thing is that while work can be accomplished by someone else, no one can replace a woman as the mother of her own children. Some people claim the social system can change that. But, can any social system replace a mother?" (op. cit., p. 92) What makes this Jusco formula slightly different from other similar exampels in the past is the fact that it is up to the workers themselves, who in actual practice are serving as the periphery, to determine whether to stay on in the peripheral segment or to become active in the core segment of the workforce. Although it may be a very rough road for a woman, there is equal opportunity for both sexes and the path is open to any woman with the ambition to climb the corporate ladder.

For any perceptive entrepreneur, of which Kojima is an example, there is another pool for supply of a possible peripheral workforce: elderly people who have retired from their previous work due to age retirement but who are still physically capable of working, willing to work, but facing extreme difficulties in today's recruitment front. When the companies that are currently striving to accomplish "weight reduction" of the corporate structure face the need to hire more workers in the future due to an upswing in the market situation, there is a strong possibility that the hiring of these elderly people will become more popular because of the same logic described by Kojima. There should be no doubt at any rate that competent entrepreneurs who are not bound to fixed notions will focus their attention on this pool of labour.

In order to clarify the reasons for saying this, I must describe some of the observations that I have made. Over recent years, people over 55 have found it extremely difficult to find a job. The situation is so bad that there are only two to three openings for every 100 job-seekers. The administrators of the school I teach at recently had one opening for a part-time job for an elderly person. I heard that some 200 applications were filed for that single post, including many coming from former department managers of companies. This is amazing especially in view of the fact that it did not offer an exactly "attractive" salary.

The typical description of an elderly job-seeker (classified as relatively "well off") would probably read like this. Having graduated from a rather well-known university, he climbed the corporate ladder to the post of department manager in a reasonable ranking company, although not the most prestigious. The severance pay he received upon retirement has been spent mostly for paying back the housing loan. But there still seems to be just enough for him and his wife to lead a modest life. If he could find a job, they would be that much more comfortable. His desire to work is partially to earn that extra bit but more than that to maintain social contact with the younger generation. And he simply wants to work for work's sake! It is quite embarrassing to hang around the house all day and do nothing. An "intellectual" and "cultivate" life style of reading and gardening does not suit him either. Loafing about doing nothing may even have negative consequences for the whole family, badly affecting his daughter's marriage. As many of his seniors have repeatedly told him, it is a joy to feel that you are appreciated while displaying the skills you have accumulated over the years although you have to be very careful not to look too pushy. Being active like that also helps prevent symptoms of senility. There seems to be a lot of psychological stress involved in becoming a part-timer at the company you used to be with. After all, you get very little stimulation from an environment you have grown accustomed to, you tend to fall into an easy-going attitude, and that hastens senility. A new job in a new environment can provide a positive stimulus. It may even be a relief to be totally detached from the old pressures and human relations. And that is also good for your ailing stomach. For someone who has risen to the level of department manager, an office where neither the work nor the human relations are related to the former company would allow him to get rid of his status con-sciousness and is perhaps more suitable for starting a second life.

As I mentioned earlier, this description illustrates the relatively "lucky ones," and we must remember that there are many in this age category who *have to* work to earn a living. The reason this example has been given here is to show that even those who went up the ladder as high as department manager strongly wish to be released from their previous status conscious-ness and be appreciated in a more discreet way. A young section manager in his mid-thirties who has such an elderly man working under him said that this elderly gentlemen processes the paper work accurately, knows how to handle visitors properly, and he finds no difficulty in having him as his sub-ordinate. As long as the managers can change their mentality and show an open-minded attitude, the elderly population that is facing serious employ-ment difficulties can prove to be the source of a fine labour force. And since most of these older people should be willing to be recruited on the basis of a yearly contract or at any rate a few years' commitment, they can form the periphery of the companies.

The problem that might arise with regard to building up the peripheral segment is, depending on the specifics of the periphery, it could lead to social injustice on a large scale or have a great impact on society. For example, as was the case with part-time factory workers in the past, if the members of the periphery consisted of the bread-winners of households, and if those members of the family were exposed to job insecurity, the impact on society in terms of injustice and consequent effects could be quite considerable. Thus, from a broader social perspective, it is desirable that the companies devise policies that would dampen such inequality and lessen the impact as much as possible.

For Japanese companies to maintain their vitality and withstand the severe international competition, it is necessary for the time being to acquire a competent core workforce. As long as long-term secured employ-ment practices are adopted for this core segment, the existence of a flexible periphery is a must. And, as things stand now, the most conceivable source of material for the periphery seems to be the increasing number of unemployed in the older age bracket most of whom are willing to work but cannot find any job. That is why I say that the formation of the periphery will move in this direction in the future. I do not look upon it as a relief measure for the elderly population. It is indeed a formula that complies with the "logic of management". When the employers can change their mentality and open their minds, a formula is available for the companies to contribute to solving the problems of the aging population while pursuing their own business logic. And, if this movement is widespread enough, it may not be entirely impossible to improve their salaries as the balance of supply and demand changes.

On the basis of the foregoing considerations, I believe that the lifetime employment system will not collapse to any great extent in the near future. Consequently, most of the Japanese management systems that have been created with the permanence of relations as a prerequisite will not, aside from partial revisions for a more effective approach, change drastically. Although there may be signs of some slight contraction of the core segment in Japanese companies, along with which there will be a tendency to expand the periphery somewhat (as seen in the case of Ricoh Co., manufacturer of business equipment, which increased the ratio of female workers), it is still necessary to maintain a functionally effective core workforce. In this sense, too, there should be no large-scale collapse of Japanese-style management.

6.3 MANAGERIAL POSTS AND AGE-GRADE PAY SYSTEM
6.3.1 Complexity of the Managerial Posts Issue

As touched upon earlier, with the shift from a high economic growth period to a low growth era, the problem of a shortage of managerial posts in Japanese companies became ever more complex and serious. During the high growth period, the age structure of a company tended to maintain a broad-based low pyramid shape due to continuous rapid expansion. Under such circumstances, there was hardly any problem about granting titles to those who accumulated long years of service to the company. It is a fact that even in those days, there were many supervisory posts and "titular posts" established not necessarily due to operational needs but merely to satisfy the status desires of the members. These included posts of which the functions were never quite clear, such as the many vice-such-and-such titles, deputy heads, assistant managers, assistant section managers, chief assistants, etc. This increase in the number of managerial posts, many of them being purely titular, provided the "foundations" for the subsequent problems of the increasing complexity of the organizational structure as well as the confusion of the command and order channels.

With the coming of the low growth period, the organizational age structure started changing rapidly. Today, in the process of the pyramid shape turning into the so-called "barrel" or "hour-glass" shape, the shortage of managerial posts has become more serious than ever.

In this context, companies are making strenuous efforts to find measures that can cope with the problem of the shortage of posts while preventing, as much as possible, a decline in employee morale. Some formulas that have been proposed include the introduction of upper age limits for managerial posts, a specialist post system, and the promotion-by-qualification system. Some of the companies have already put these measures into practice. More recently, there have been companies that even began studying the possiblity of adopting the "merit system" (as opposed to the seniority system) for employees over 35 years old.

At the same time, as concerns the "bloated managerial posts" that have become too large in number and too nominal in nature, questions are being raised regarding the eligibility of some of the people in these posts for overtime pay and membership in the union. These problems surfaced when the Ministry of Labour issued an official notification to the financial institutions and finance-related trade associations throughout Japan in February and March 1977. According to the newspapers, those holding low-ranking supervisory posts such as deputy section managers and deputy branch managers were withdrawn from managerial treatment and were to be granted overtime pay in lieu of their conventional "managerial post allowance". *Nihon Keizai Shimbun* (June 18, 1977) reported that the number of bank employees who were declassified as "managers" in this sense totalled some 30,000 for the thirteen city banks during the months of April and May. The resulting increase in personnel costs ranged from 300 to 500 million yen a year for each bank. The Ministry of Labour is said to have stated that it "plans to gradually guide the other industries into observing a stricter definition of managerial posts". The article also mentioned that this sort of measure is creating another type of complication in the field of personnel management in that those who have been stripped of their managerial treatment feel that despite the increase in their overall salaries, their pride has been hurt, thus having an adverse effect on their morale. So, in addition to the shortage of managerial posts, pressure is starting to be exerted from the viewpoint of the application of the Labour Standards Law.

Various measures being tried out by companies in response to such circumstances have been widely reported in the newspapers, economic and business magazines, and survey results. Therefore, in the following section, I would like to clarify why, bearing in mind the relations between Japanese-style management and the psychological foundations, a "shortage of managerial posts," something that could not become a major issue in American and European organizations, is regarded as a major issue in Japan.

Furthermore, the future direction of the countermeasures for this problem will be sought, once again in connection with the psychological foundations.

6.3.2 Shortage of Posts and Age-grade Pay System: The Psychological Foundations

In a sense, this serious shortage of posts arises for a very simple reason, the cause being the style of Japanese management itself (which is based on the concept of age-grade or seniority), and the employees' "expectations" of winning a position within the organization nurtured by such a style of management. Thus, the shortage of posts could easily be solved by abolishing the age-grade system. The fact that, despite this simple formula, the issue has become one of the major concerns for the employers goes to show that it is not as simple as all that.

The explanation of why the solution of this problem is extremely difficult is as follows. In the forementioned example of the banks, we saw that the re-classification of those in the low-echelon (and titular) managerial posts caused a sharp increase in personnel costs, on the one hand, while acting to lower the morale of the employees, on the other. As was reflected by this phenomenon, the age-grade pay system under Japanese-style management has for a long time provided a low-cost yet effective incentive system. And, to date, there has emerged no effective alternative system that the employers can feel assured of to replace the conventional age-grade system.

As was shown by the analysis in Chapter 3, the age-grade pay system has functioned effectively over the years because of existence of solid psychological foundations supporting it, such as the unique egalitarianism among the Japanese, the status awareness of being particularly sensitive to one's position within the group, and the unique concept of man's capabilities in which the evaluation of one's capabilities tends to be directly linked to that person's value as a human being. It is the existence of these psychological foundations that seem to be strongly obstructing the possible attempts to solve the problem by introducing a Western-style merit system.

Although the age-grade pay system has, on the whole, been "conformable to the Japanese mentality" and has been "serving as a rare incentive system displaying an excellent effect," the degree of effect has differed from one company to another. And, since many other factors are involved, it is not as if the system has been functioning well in all Japanese companies. Still, when we look at the age-grade pay system as one of the patterns that struck roots deeply in Japanese management, it can be seen to be a formula that has been cleverly designed to conform to the Japanese management climate.

The shortage of managerial posts, an issue that has become increasingly noticeable very recently, is as serious and complicated as it is because it clashes sharply with the age-grade pay system. If, as many analysts of business management have pointed out in the past, the age-grade pay system were obsolete, disfunctional, and thus should be reformed as soon as possible, the problem would be that much simpler and could not have developed into a major issue. If that had been the case, the problem would be reduced to the question of temporary confusion and acclimatization accompanying any transition as was the situation when Japan switched to the metric system from its traditional scale of measurement. The actual problem of the shortage of managerial posts is not as simple as all that and involves delving into the deep psychology of the Japanese people.

6.3.3 Coping with the Problem of Shortage of Posts

Since the issue of a shortage of managerial posts includes serious and complex aspects, the solution to the problem is by no means easy. Nevertheless, pressure from the environment is mounting and the companies, each under its own philosophy, are going through great pains in trying to come up with countermeasures. Hideyuki Kudo, a columnist with the *Nihon Keizai Shimbun,* comments as follows in a paper dealing with this point.

"The shortage of managerial posts has become a source of grave concern for the personnel administrators. Already, this problem has cast dark shadows on some of the companies. But the problem will get even more serious in the future. ... Although there is no *magic formula* for solving this problem, companies have begun *groping* for solutions through attempts such as raising morale by revising the titles for some positions and qualification categories or by establishing a non-managerial promotion ladder." (Italics added by the author) ("Posuto Fusoku Jidai no Jinji Kanri," *Nihon Keizai Shimbun,* May 8, 1978)

What is interesting in the process of this search for countermeasures is that there are very few examples of stressing a Western-style "merit system". To the contrary, most of the efforts seem to be directed towards solving the problem while somehow maintaining the age-grade pay concept. For example, the method of creating many posts reading something like "such-and-such" and other equally ambiguous posts, is a step taken in the past within the framework of the age-grade pay scheme. The establishment of an upper age limit for managerial posts aims at providing opportunities to as many members of the organization as possible to assume managerial posts, thus providing them with satisfaction. The specialist post system is nothing but a scheme to grant those who will not assume managerial posts some other status and feeling of pride. And the qualification system is nothing but the introduction of titles based on ranking by qualification which can be given out to as many people as needed, instead of granting adminstrative posts which are quite limited in number. Obviously, depending on how they are implemented, some of these systems can be employed on the basis of the merit system. However, in actual practice, they are being developed as one form of Japanese style "merit system" (a capability-oriented pay scheme)* under which differentials are slowly incorporated with the age-grade concept still serving as the basic backbone.

In my view, out of these various ideas and efforts there will develop a formula that conforms to the psychology of the Japanese, that is effective in enhancing worker morale, and also that enables a smooth implementation of the overall management system. As long as the psychological traits of the Japanese do not change drastically, the basics of Japanese-style pay system based on the evaluation of one's capabilities* will not change that much.

At this point, I would like to offer some of my views on the question of the introduction of the Western-style merit system, a system that does not place too much stress on age.

As we already saw, Japanese tend to be particularly sensitive about wage and other treatment differentials. Moreover, concern over the social prestige of the group one is affiliated with as well as one's position within the hierarchy of the group is also strongly felt by most Japanese. As *Hideyuki Kudo* mentions, the latter is especially true when one's position in his group also reflects his social status. Furthermore, most Japanese who are extremely conscious of senior-junior relationships spend a major portion of their life with one business organization until the prescribed retirement age under the lifetime employment system. Under such circumstances, the introduction of an American or European-style merit system, which does not take into consideration the seniority factor too much, could create a very harsh atmosphere. In Western societies where there is relative freedom to change one's job, when a person is not convinced of his evaluation, he can look for another company to work for where he will perhaps feel happier. Or, he could even change professions by acquiring a new skill, learning a new language, etc.

In Japanese society, however, switching jobs is extremely difficult because of the lifetime employment system. When meritocracy practices are introduced into such an environment, many organization members, aside from a handful of elites, would be driven to the wall with no escape exists. One can claim all one wants that consideration is shown in conducting personnel evaluations. But essentially, the evalution is a unilateral operation. As a result, many of the Japanese people who attach great importance to their position within the organization will be driven into a situation where they will have to face the frustration of their life being a failure. Of course,

---

* See Chapter 3, Section 3.2.2-(ii).

even in the past, very capable persons were eventually granted suitable posts and thus enjoyed better treatment than other less competent men. But even in such cases, care has been taken by keeping the salary differentials as small as possible, providing ample time for all parties concerned to get used to the new differentials, or relocating the "losers" in the promotion race to a different department. Excepting cases where abilities can be objectively measured and are clear to all parties concerned, the introduction of a Western-type merit system in the Japanese management climate would create emotional and unsound human relations within the organizations. Consequently, there is a great danger that companies and other forms of organizations could become very uncongenial places for their members.

The survey by Nippon Recruit Center offers some very interesting results on this point (See Table 6.1). It shows that the larger the size of the company, the more serious the problem of "morale management of non-promoted members." In the current situation in which Japanese companies have become as powerful as they are, and especially in consideration of the fact that the Japanese people are being criticized for working too hard, it is desirable that a company maintain a pleasant atmosphere for the workers so long as it can maintain its vitality.

From the standpoint of the employers, too, the introduction of the merit system implies a number of problems. Generally speaking, American and European organizations are supported by a Western-type awareness of contractual relations and obligations, function on the basis of clearly specified tasks allocated to each individual, and possess relative freedom (as compared with Japan) to replace any undesirable segment of the workforce through dismissal. To the contrary, Japanese organizations rely on good will and cooperation among the members and it is almost impossible to simply dismiss incompetent workers who show no signs of making any efforts. So, in a Japanese company, it is far more effective to try to raise the overall strength of the company by preventing members from losing their enthusiasm and giving encouragement to the weaker elements in the workforce, rather than for a handufl of powerful elites to work like the dickens and take command of the whole entity.

The introduction of the merit system would act as a counterforce against this Japanese approach of upgrading the overall strength. It is conceivable to think of an ideal situation whereby the introduction of the merit system would motivate all of the members to work even harder and as a result everyone still remained on more or less the same level. But this does not seem too realistic. And it would not do anything to solve the problem of the shortage of managerial posts. In any event, it seems that the hasty introduction of a Western-style merit system, based on ideas that the elites would tend to advocate, could entail great dangers.

Table 6.1 Three Biggest Problems Concerning Promotions
A Breakdown by Company Size
(Figures in parentheses indicate the number of companies)

N = 443

Company Size (No. of employees)	1st	2nd	3rd
Total	Lack of appropriate evaluation methods (156)	Morale problems concerning non-promoted members (113)	Evaluation methods not standardized (103)
249 and less	Lack of appropriate evaluation methods (32)	Evaluation affected by say of influential individuals (23)	Morale problems concerning non-promoted members (17)
250–499	Lack of appropriate evaluation methods (31)	Evaluation affected by say of influential individuals (20)	Evaluation methods not standardized (19)
500–999	Lack of appropriate evaluation methods (42)	Morale problems concerning non-promoted members (26)	Evaluation methods not standardized (26)
1000–2999	Morale problems concerning non-promoted members (35)	Lack of appropriate evaluation methods (33)	Evaluation methods not standardized (29)
3000 and above	Morale problems concerning non-promoted members (20)	Lack of appropriate evaluation methods (18)	Evaluation methods not standardized (14)

Source: Report on Promotion Surveys, Nippon Recruit Center, April 1978.

6.3.4 Prospects Regarding the Shortage

Finally, I would like to offer some observations concerning the future of this problem of the shortage of managerial posts. As has already been explained in detail, it is clear that at the core of this problem lies the question of the unique Japanese concept of status. In other words, under the age-grade pay system that conforms with the unique sense of egalitarianism, concept of capabilities, and status awareness, intra-organizational ranking that satisfies the status desires of the members has, for some time now, been linked directly with the managerial posts that are limited in number. This is the crux of the matter. Similar problems are detected in universities where the chair system is adopted, such as in medical schools.

Basically, two approaches are conceivable as countermeasures for solving this problem. First, is the method of intensifying competition for the *limited number* of posts. The other is to dissociate the ranking of members within organizations from the managerial posts, which are obviously limited in number, so that there is no limit to the supply of status positions. This is similar to the step taken by universities that have done away with the chair system so that there is no limit to the number of professorships granted, meaning that anyone who meets certain qualifications can become a professor.

Generally speaking, I believe that it is desirable to respect the status awareness of the Japanese as much as possible. Ideally, it is desirable to have an organization where all the members can work with confidence and pride, without being looked down upon by their colleagues, and find joy in working within that organization. With the Japanese who attach value to good will and respect from their colleagues, forceful "carrot and stick" methods using money and position as tools are not necessarily required.

In reality, organizations do have to provide various incentives. I believe, however, that for the time being and as long as the organizations do not lose their vitality or slow down, the differentials should be kept small. The Japanese companies can probably maintain their vitality better that way than if they introduced the merit system. The employees, too, would find their working environment a more pleasant one that way.

In view of these analyses, I feel that in coping with the problem of the shortage of managerial posts faced by many companies today, it is desirable to maintain the "Japanese-style (capability-oriented) merit system"* under which slight differentials are introduced gradually into the continual promotion system. Means for coping with the conflict

---

* See Chapter 3, Section 3.2.2 (ii), p. 60.

between the shortage of posts and respecting the status awareness of the Japanese can vary depending on subjective factors such as the history and nature of business of each company as well as on external factors as environmental conditions. It should, however, be possible to separate the intra-organizational ranking, salaries, and managerial posts from each other. It is important to bear in mind that the crux of the problem concerning managerial posts is the question of status.

The fact that a Japanese worker will be absolutely frustrated over the smallest difference in salary with his colleague of the same seniority (even if that difference amounts to the price of a couple of packs of cigarettes a month), or that he will be dying to assume the post of section manager even if that means a considerable decrease in his take-home pay, goes to show that basically these are connected with their "status" within the organization. By separating status, salary, and managerial posts, various problems facing Japanese management today can be coped with. First of all, members of the organization will climb the ladder of intra-organizational ranking, step by step, under the continual promotion system. In that process, it is inevitable that some differentials are introduced when elements desirable to the company, such as enthusiasm for work and contribution to the organization, are evaluated. In connection with this, it is hoped that opportunities can be offered subsequently for others to try again and display their competence.

Salaries should be determined primarily on the basis of the employees' livelihood needs and their share of labour. Their position, i.e. their contribution to the organization, should also be evaluated and determined. Since status and salaries are dissociated, it would not be surprising that someone whose status is low but who has a heavy work load would be receiving a high salary. Or, it could happen that after having reached a certain status or age, that person's take-home pay could stagnate or if necessary even go down. By incorporating the selective early retirement system into this, it will be easier to raise the compulsory retirement age, saving the companies from future financial collapse caused by heavy severance pay and/or high salary burdens of older workers.

What remains difficult here is the separation of status from managerial posts. But it is by no means totally impossible, because Japanese organizations do not function so much around the concept and practice of authority and orders but more on the basis of mutual trust and consensus between the members. The role of the managers under this system will inevitably change considerably. If the dynamism of the organization should be reduced somewhat by it, the managers of each department and section can be given different types of roles to maintain the vitality. It will be a matter of each company adapting to the given situation. In this way, it should also be possible to grant the managerial posts to those who are most qualified for those positions.

Let me give one example. In many of the universities that do not adopt the chair system, there are four broad professional categories: professors, assistant professors, lecturers, and research assistants. The pay schedules of these categories are different from each other but the differences are quite minimal. On the other hand, there are the "line" positions such as dean, chief librarian, chairman of the instruction affairs committee, chairman of the entrance examination committee, etc. Although titles like the dean and chief librarian are accompanied by some status prestige, there are not too many volunteers for the posts due to the heavy burden of work they imply. So, they are usually rotated. Serving as chairman of a committee is almost interpreted as a "tax" faculty members have to pay in order to "survive" in the organization. When it comes to a post like the head of the student affairs department, because of its particularly heavy work load, most universities find their faculty members displaying their modesty and forcing it on one another. Once they attain a professorship, most university teachers quickly lose any aspiration for further status. Although the value of a professorship has decreased considerably in terms of social prestige, this title which carries a long tradition and is universally accepted does still satisfy one's desire for status. So, after that point, not too many want to become dean or president.

I am not trying to say that such a mechanism of the universities will serve as very useful material for companies. But the fact that this type of an organization does exist in Japanese society in great numbers suggests that the structure of most Japanese companies where the intra-organizational status is directly linked with the managerial post is not the only conceivable form. What is crucial when coping with the problem of a shortage of managrial posts is the question of how to establish a "prestigious status ladder" that is detached from the "line" or managerial posts. One of the important points here will be the promotion path leading to the executive's chair. Hideyuki Kudo's remarks go to the heart of the matter. "There is no reason why higher posts in a company should be occupied by administrative managers. Project managers, strategy planners, specialist workers, and expert staff should also be given opportunities for reaching high-ranking posts. This could open the path for them to possibly make it to an executive's chair." (Kudo, ibid.)

The unique system of management often referred to as "Japanese-style management" is, as we have seen, faced with several serious problems and pressure is mounting to cope with these issues. Nevertheless, I believe that solutions to the problems will be sought while basically moving along the lines that have been followed so far, with the introduction of a number of modifications here and there. The limits of Japanese-style management are the limits of the *current system,* not the limits of a system conformable to the Japanese people and society.

1. RESPON TO GROUP
2. GOODWILL OR CO-WORKERS
3. PERSONAL GOAL + INFLUENCE
4. POWER OVER CAREER OR STAFF